Interiors Now

images
Publishing

Published in Australia in 2004 by
The Images Publishing Group Pty Ltd
ABN 89 059 734 431
6 Bastow Place, Mulgrave, Victoria, 3170, Australia
Telephone: +61 3 9561 5544 Facsimile: +61 3 9561 4860
books@images.com.au
www.imagespublishinggroup.com

National Library of Australia
Cataloguing-in-Publication data

Interiors now

Includes index.
ISBN 1 920744 67 3

1. Interior decoration. 2. Interior decoration—Pictorial works.
3. Decoration and ornament, Architectural. I. Title.

729

Coordinating editors: Daniel Pavlovits and Joe Boschetti
Designed by The Graphic Image Studio Pty Ltd, Mulgrave, Australia
www.tgis.com.au
Printed by Everbest Printing Co. Ltd. in Hong Kong/China

Front cover: T-House by Jakob McFarlane
Photography: Nicolas Borel
Rear cover: O'Neill Guesthouse by Lubowicki Lanier Architecture
Photography: Erich Koyama

IMAGES has included on its Website a page for special notices in
relation to this and its other publications. Please visit this site:
www.imagespublishinggroup.com

IMAGES is pleased to add Interiors Now to its compendium of design
and architectural publications. We wish to thank all participating
firms for their valuable contribution to this publication.

Contents

Corporate

Hospitality and Public

Residential

Retail

Index

680 Second Street

San Francisco, California, USA

CCS Architecture

This is a commercial tenant improvement for a 60,000-square-foot space for a high-tech financial services firm. The firm wanted a showcase office for its San Francisco headquarters, which would house a mix of corporate financial offices, technology developers, and administration.

The site is a recently renovated four-story structure with a garage located in a former dry-dock facility. Set up for multi-tenancy, it had a relatively small floor plate, which is not easily suited to a single tenant. The clients wanted to foster communication between floors and departments, as well as to allow for a flexible open office environment that would allow for growth and expansion. The solution was to connect the floors through a central circulation spine in the form of a stair. This penetrated the various floors on one axis, and stacked program around that axis-spine on all of the floors.

The top floor is reserved for conferencing and meeting space, concentrating major facilities such as break rooms, conferencing, and arterial support around the 'spine.' It stretches from the ground floor lobby to the uppermost floor in a direct line, with support located centrally around it. The server room, built to cantilever over the main lobby, stretches the program in violation of the perimeter enclosure yet maintains its relationship to the spine.

Above: Main lobby/entrance with server room above

Above left: Internal linking stair with break area beyond

Above: Detail at handrail

Opposite: Above main
lobby/entrance with
server room above

680 Second Street

Right: Detail of stair at fourth floor with stainless-mesh wrap and conference room beyond

Photography: Michael O'Callahan

CCS Architecture
44 McLea Court
San Francisco, California, 94103
USA
Tel: 415-864-2800
Fax: 415-864-2850
Email: info@ccs-architecture.com

CCS Architecture, the design studio of Cass Calder Smith, is dedicated to excellence in Architecture and Design. Since it's inception in 1990, CCS has designed a diverse range of public and private buildings and interiors for living, working, eating, and more. The firm has gained international acclaim for the architectural and commercial success of restaurant projects, while the uniqueness of residential, commercial, and mixed-use projects has met with an unusual degree of owner satisfaction and media praise.

CCS seeks to explore opportunities of maximum potential and express them at a scale appropriate to each project. The work is firmly based in the modernist idiom where innovation and creativity are balanced by common sense and experience. The firm is known for creating projects with exceptional spatial and material qualities, and for providing outstanding professional service.

AC Martin Partners Office

Los Angeles, California, USA

AC Martin Partners

This design for AC Martin Partners' own offices in the central business district of Los Angeles is the result of an internal design charette to generate design ideas and direction. Throughout the process, many members of the firm's design and engineering departments worked on the conception and execution of the office space.

The partners sought an open, loft-like space to foster more fluid inter-departmental communication and to energize creative collaboration. The new one-floor work space (the previous offices were on three separate floors) needed to accommodate 100 employees in architecture, planning, engineering, marketing, and administration.

Occupying the twelfth floor of an office tower in the Los Angeles central business district, a tower which was originally designed by ACMP, the location ensures the firm's proximity to civic clients and reinforces its position as community advocate leaders.

The dominating design and functional motif is the Unistrut, a commutable hanging system that holds wood, cement boards, glass, and lighting. Open slats of wood paneling, cement boards and sheets of frosted glass demarcate the open plan with areas where specific events take place, such as private offices, conference rooms, and communal spaces. The creative and efficient use of new systems and materials is also a way for the firm to demonstrate its leadership in offering effective design solutions to its clients.

The firm's commitment to sustainability and new materials exploration is evidenced by the long-wearing flooring material that combines characteristics of carpeting and resilient flooring. The low-loop Metafloor uses 50 percent less nylon, translating into a 50 percent reduction in oil consumption.

Left: Unistrut system defines zones of usage in open-office plan

Above: Wood, glass, and cement board are used to vary and experiment with materials

Left: Design principal's office is easily accessible to junior designers

Top: Sliding 'barn doors' allow access and openness

Above: Lobby displays full range of materials found throughout office

Above: Colored light system allows architects to experiment with different effects

Photography: John Edward Linden

AC Martin Partners
444 South Flower Street
Los Angeles, California, 90071
USA
Tel: +1 213 683 1900
Fax: +1 213 614 6002
Email: marketing@acmartin.com

AC Martin Partners, Inc. (ACMP), is an integrated architecture, engineering, and planning firm with a long-standing tradition of creating environments that have had significant impacts upon their surroundings through craft, integrity, and social responsibility. The Los Angeles-based firm's wide range of clients includes corporations, government agencies, developers, cultural organizations, and educational institutions. Recent and upcoming projects include California Environmental Protection Agency (Sacramento), Chapman University Master Plan, high schools for LA Unified School District, Grand Avenue Master Plan, Ventura County Museum of History and Art, RiverPark Community Plan, LA City Hall Restoration, Fresno County Appellate Court, and the National Ignition Facility at Lawrence Livermore National Laboratory. Founded in 1906 by Albert C. Martin Sr., the firm continues to shape the Southern Californian region, creating some of the area's most well-known, user-focused, innovative, sustainable, and beautiful landmarks for the 21st century.

Albertina, Extension and Renovation

Vienna, Austria

Steinmayr & Mascher Architects

The Albertina palace is renowned worldwide for housing perhaps the most significant single collection of graphics and prints. Located in Vienna next to the Hofburg in the city's historical center, the museum has a multi-layered history of construction, dating back almost 800 years. The current project's brief was to intervene in this history and design an extension to this landmark building.

Since 1980, there had been ongoing discussions about redesigning the building's complex entry area and improving its technical services. In 1993, an architecture competition also gave directives for the re-establishment of the entrance over the old ramp on the building's southwest side, as well as provision for a modern storage facility for the prints and graphics archives, and research rooms for academics.

The winning project from Erich Steinmayr and Friedrich Mascher presented an optimal expansion of the bastion between the ramp and the subsurface levels of the building without interfering with the historical façades. The key to their plan was to shorten the old ramp and gain a 60-foot width between the building and the Burggarten greenhouse in the palace grounds. The extension of interior spaces reflects the architects' approach to both historical conservation and modern intervention.

Below: New research area
Photographer: Anna Blau

Above: Transition zone
between new and old buildings

Photographer: Bruno Klomfar

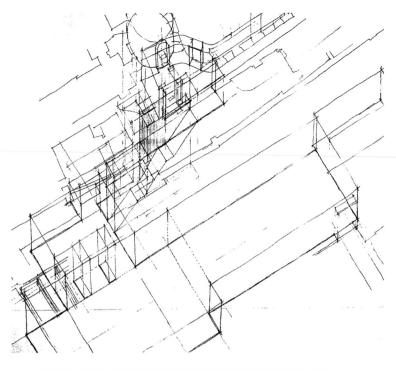

Top left: Main entrance and foyer
Photographer: Bruno Klomfar

Top right: Sketch

Above: Research area with view
to garden courtyard

Left: Hallway to research building
with basement storage zones
Photographer: Anna Blau

Above: Daylight
penetration into new
extension

Photographer: Anna Blau

Steinmayr & Mascher Architects
Mariahilferstrasse 89/27
A-1060 Vienna
Austria
Telephone: +43 1 581 1192
Facsimile: +43 1 587 8766
Email: mascher@netway.at

Erich Steinmayr and Friedrich Mascher have separate architecture practices in Vienna, Vienna. They have collaborated on projects since 1993, when they submitted a joint proposal for the redevelopment, extension, and renovation of the famous Albertina prints archive and gallery in Vienna. Individually, they have taught as guest lecturers at various schools of architecture in Europe. They enter architecture competitions regularly and have completed a number of joint projects in Vienna and across Europe, while maintaining individual practices.

Del Monte
San Francisco, California, USA
IA Interior Architects

Del Monte asked IA to provide design services for 105,000 square feet of office space for the relocation of its headquarters into a historic landmark structure in San Francisco. The design challenge was to both reflect the company's 100-year heritage and address today's business needs.

To support the historical nature of the project, the design makes use of existing brick walls, concrete columns and beams, and exposed mechanical elements. IA's design also gave special attention to restoring as many original features as possible.

In the carpet, upholstery, and wall finishes, primary accent colors represent the tomatoes, corn, and peas of Del Monte's food products. The general area carpet complements the rough concrete and brick finishes. Sliding glass doors at perimeter offices let in natural light, so that no employee is more than 20 feet away from a source of daylight or a view. To meet a requirement that many workers should be relocated from offices to open work areas, IA designed partially enclosed perimeter work areas defined by corrugated plastic panels that provide visual and acoustical privacy.

Below: Reception area and conference suite

Above: Employee café with terrace and views of bay and bridge

Right: Semi-private perimeter offices

Opposite: Interior corridor at offices and open work space

Del Monte

Above: Main reception area
overlooking building atrium

Photography: David Wakely Photography

IA Interior Architects

350 California Street, Suite 1500
San Francisco, California, 94104
USA
Tel: +1 415 434 3305
Fax: +1 415 434 0330
Email: k.vanert@interiorarchitects.com

IA Interior Architects is the only global architectural firm to concentrate exclusively on interior architecture. The firm's focus on interiors drove the creation of the company and continues to be its driving force.

Established in 1984, IA has an 18-year track record of delivering successful office interior design projects to a wide range of clients in the United States and internationally. IA today has offices in 13 American cities, London and Shanghai. Its corporate headquarters are in San Francisco.

When IA was founded, it was decided that its architectural practice would be from the inside out, as interior architects. IA Interior Architects believes it takes a special expertise to design an exceptional interior space. As interior architects the firm's approach to design is exclusively focused on how the aesthetics and organization of a space can reflect brand image, improve efficiency and productivity, reduce churn and increase employee satisfaction. A chief goal of the firm is to support its clients' business objectives by enhancing the design and performance of their work environments.

DZ Bank

Berlin, Germamy

Gehry Partners, LLP

The DZ Bank Building is a mixed-use building comprising a commercial component which houses the Berlin headquarters of DZ Bank and a residential component consisting of 39 apartments. The building's commercial component is oriented towards Pariser Platz and the Brandenburg Gate, while the residential component is oriented towards Behrenstrasse. Both the Pariser Platz façade and the Behrenstrasse façade are clad in a buff-colored limestone that matches the Brandenburg Gate. The façades are scaled independently from one another, so that the proportions of both are appropriate to the immediate urban area within which they each exist.

A high-volume foyer immediately inside the main entry offers a view into the building's large interior atrium, which features a curving glass ceiling and a curving glass floor. A timber-clad arcade leads to the office elevator lobbies, which are located on either side of the atrium. Office spaces are organized around the atrium, and are oriented inward to take advantage of the natural light that floods through the glass ceiling.

The building's primary conference hall is located within a highly sculptural shell in the center of the glass floor of the atrium. Clad in stainless steel on the exterior and timber on the interior, the hall appears to float in the fluid depth of the space.

Below: Glass roof structure

Below: Section

Bottom left: View from gallery level

Bottom right: 'Horse's Head' structure at night

Opposite: Entrance 'Horse's Head' structure

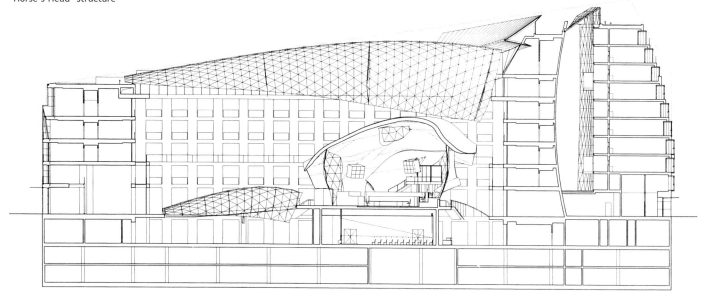

DZ Bank

Left: Glimpse of 'Horse's Head' structure
Photography: Roland Halbe

Gehry Partners, LLP

1520-B Cloverfield Boulevard
Santa Monica, California, 90404
USA
Telephone: +1 310 828 6088
Facsimile: +1 310 828 2098
Email: info@foga.com

Gehry Partners is a full-service firm with broad international experience in museum, theater performance, institutional, commercial, and residential projects. Located in Los Angeles, California, Gehry Partners has a staff of over 120 people.

The firm employs a network of sophisticated CAD workstations in the development of projects and in the translation of design ideas into the technical documents required for construction. The firm uses CATIA, a three-dimensional computer-modelling program originally designed for the aerospace industry, to document designs and to rationalize the bidding, fabrication, and construction process. CATIA is supplemented by more traditional two-dimensional CAD programs.

The combination of model building and mock-up capabilities, materials research, and the application of advanced computer systems and construction techniques allows Gehry Partners to develop designs in a rational process, that reach beyond the traditional limits of architecture.

Finnish Embassy

Canberra, Australia

Arkkitehtuuritsto Hirvonen—Huttunen

Arkkitehtuuritoimisto Hirvonen—Huttunen: Vesa Huttunen and Nikolas Davies
MGT Architects: Romaldo Giurgola, Tim Halden Brown and Robert Thorne

In 1997, the Finnish State arranged an architectural competition for a new embassy building in Canberra, the administrative capital of Australia.

The embassy's vestibule spaces and staircase overlook an entrance courtyard through a glass atrium. The building's main glass façade provides a display window for the embassy's day-to-day activities. Diffused sunlight penetrates the offices inside through projecting strip windows. The façade's internal and external surfaces are made from stainless-steel plates with a rolled finish, which reflect its surroundings. These themes are repeated in the building's other internal spaces. Different materials have been divided with glass walls and doors, while the mesh ceiling, cutting through the whole building, unites the various spaces. The building technology has been left visible on purpose and installations have not been encased. For instance, the elevator gear can be viewed through the glass walls on either side of the elevator's sliding door.

The embassy's interior materials form a contrast to the cool appearance of its external façades. The warm tones of three different varieties of eucalyptus dominate the internal space. The main staircase in the entrance hall is a freestanding jarrah tower, which can be closed off by doors. The floors of the building are of solid pale eucalyptus. Almost all of the walls between the offices have been made in the form of wooden built-in cupboards for additional storage.

Below: Ambassador's room faces three different directions

Right: Outer wall separated from concrete structures by glass roof and floor

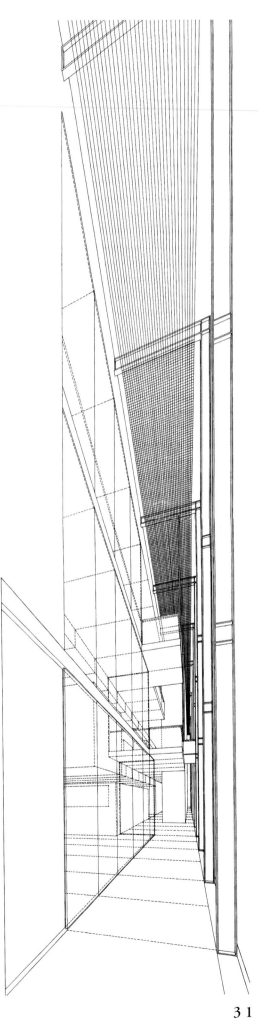

Above: Three-story atrium
unites spaces vertically

Right: Building perspective

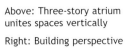

Left: Kitchen unit and toilet facilities can be sealed off by sliding doors

Below: Traditional Finnish sauna, with apache wood benches

Photography: John Gollings

Arkkitehtuuritsto Hirvonen—Huttunen
Arkkitehtuuritoimisto Hirvonen—Huttunen: Vesa Huttunen and Nikolas Davies
MGT Architects: Romaldo Giurgola, Tim Halden Brown and Robert Thorne
Laivakatu 3
00150 Helsinki
Finland
Telephone: 358 9 6224710
Facsimile: 358 9 658910
Email: hh.arkkitehdit@kolumbus.fi

Arkkitehtuuritoimisto Hirvonen-Huttunen (Hirvonen-Huttunen Architects) is based in Helsinki, Finland. The firm was founded in 1992 and since its inception, it has won several architectural design competitions in Finland and overseas.

The practice's projects are multifaceted with a core of designs for residential housing, and extensions and renovations. A larger commercial and award-winning project is the Finnish Embassy building in Canberra, Australia, which was completed recently. Apart from its core projects, the firm has also designed a number of bridges, one being built in Finland.

Fotouhi Alonso Associates

Culver City, California, USA

Shubin + Donaldson Architects

Fotouhi Alonso Associates is a 20-year-old full-service advertising agency for the 'New Marketplace,' working with Internet companies, as well as traditional companies that are reinventing themselves. Its clients include CitySearch.com, MSNBC, First Federal Bank, China Airlines, and GetPlugged.com.

The design team was asked to build a work space for 25 staff that would fundamentally reflect the client's work in the world of the Internet and technology. The large open sense of the space of this former industrial facility has been maintained by the designers. The architects followed the bones of the building to create space and maintain light throughout the office. The existing steel frame and sawtooth-structured façade define the window-front conference room. Original structural wood beams lend character throughout the office in tandem with the ochre-colored soffit that runs through the space, concealing industrial ducts and electrical wiring cables.

Large Lumicite and aluminum panels run throughout the office, and define individual spaces. This inspired touch also serves a dual function of creating privacy and keeping light flowing throughout the large loft-like space in which windows exist only on the perimeter walls. Besides adding light, the translucent walls provide support for the soffit structure. The open frames also accommodate shelving for various private offices and casual spaces.

Workstations are defined by homosote board and vertical red panels with varnished work surfaces. Furniture is kept minimal with red seating accents. Concrete floors were maintained with original 'designs' left by previous occupants over the years.

The glass-enclosed conference room is sited to the sawtooth front of the building. Concrete floors run directly into the glass storefront of the building.

Right: Main conference room faces front of building

Above: Custom
workstations are kept
spare and simple

Right: Aluminum structure
of light walls is used as
shelving storage

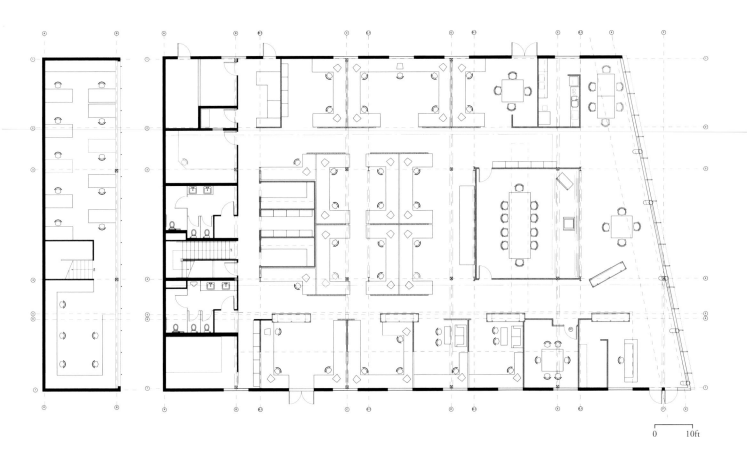

Top: Floor plan

Above: Light-box walls and diagonal beams create a rhythm down the hall

Left: Reception area introduces themes of light, grid, and space

Right: Architects kept original wood beams for industrial feeling

Photography: Tom Bonner

Shubin + Donaldson Architects

3834 Willat Avenue
Culver City, California, 90232
USA
Tel: +1 310 204 0688
Fax: +1 310 204 0219
Email: rshubin@sandarc.com

Shubin + Donaldson Architects, established in 1990 in Culver City, California, is an inventive firm whose current work includes a diverse listing of commercial and residential projects ranging from entertainment-business studios, creative offices and retail stores, to community centers and custom residences. Russell Shubin, AIA, and Robin Donaldson, AIA, have distinguished principals of the 'branded environment,' which they apply to their clients in technology, advertising, Internet, and creative production. Their approach addresses the characteristics of branding, function, adaptability, and anti-hierarchical structures, which are designed with clear interior concepts and commitment to good design as a means to achieve business goals. Their residential work is context and client driven and exudes contemporary living.

Fuel Design & Production

Santa Monica, California, USA

Shubin + Donaldson Architects

Known for its cutting-edge computer animation and digital design, Fuel Design & Production enjoys a converted 8000-square-foot loft space. The environment is both fun and serious, thus reflecting the working culture of the company. The architects combined and contrasted the basic raw industrial look of the original warehouse.

The studio features transparent conduits to carry computer wiring and cables that emphasize how the latest technology functions at Fuel. Translucent panels are also featured throughout the space, not only allowing light to pass through, but also acting as screens upon which Fuel can project changing images of its work. Much of the main shell of the existing warehouse was left intact and exposed, including the concrete and terrazzo floors. Each section or office was designed as a self-contained space within the larger building, creating the feeling of an interior village of buildings.

Right: Executive's office is anything but typical

Opposite: Industrial, off-the-shelf materials amplify raw space

Above left: Large areas of translucent walls double as projection screens

Above: Muted red and blue are main accent colors

Left: 'Info bar' carries electrical conduit throughout office

Above: One of several 'war rooms'—small conference rooms along hallway

Above right: Translucent walls glow with indirect light in computer-intensive space

Photography: Farshid Assassi

Shubin + Donaldson Architects

3834 Willat Avenue
Culver City, California, 90232
USA
Tel: +1 310 204 0688
Fax: +1 310 204 0219
Email: rshubin@sandarc.com

Shubin + Donaldson Architects, established in 1990 in Culver City, California, is an inventive firm whose current work includes a diverse listing of commercial and residential projects ranging from entertainment-business studios, creative offices and retail stores, to community centers and custom residences. Russell Shubin, AIA, and Robin Donaldson, AIA, have distinguished principals of the 'branded environment,' which they apply to their clients in technology, advertising, Internet, and creative production. Their approach addresses the characteristics of branding, function, adaptability, and anti-hierarchical structures, which are designed with clear interior concepts and commitment to good design as a means to achieve business goals. Their residential work is context and client driven and exudes contemporary living.

Geiger International Showroom
Chicago, USA
VOA Associates Incorporated

Geiger International contracted VOA to design its showroom when the company relocated to the top floor of a turn-of-the-century warehouse in Chicago. The 7100-square-foot showroom was designed in close collaboration with Geiger International's president, John Geiger. VOA won the project on the strength of its 'theatre-in-the-round' concept presentation.

John Geiger wanted the showroom to merge old and new worlds while providing an educational center for his clientele. He also requested a visual reference directly to the city of Chicago. The layout and design that VOA developed achieved all these goals with style.

At key junctures throughout the showroom, clean drywall areas, representing modern architectural environments where Geiger furniture products ultimately reside, meet the rusticated loft areas, evoking the history of the craftsmanship of the furniture itself. As guests enter the space they are greeted on one side by the Geiger identity, and on the other by a visual timeline of Geiger's history.

Four 15-foot by 15-foot 'casegood' display areas, where John Geiger wanted to be able to demonstrate various price-points of furniture options, are delineated not by walls but by ceiling planes and space layout. The materials library is the dynamic 'theatre-in-the-round' space, where the soft curved wall, with its multiple sliding doors and cabinetry, provides either a backdrop to the furniture or an interactive, educational resource area.

Outside the windows of the primary circulation area, an elevated train runs past the showroom, connecting employees and guests to the bloodline of John Geiger's beloved Chicago.

Left: Chicago connection through window/wall

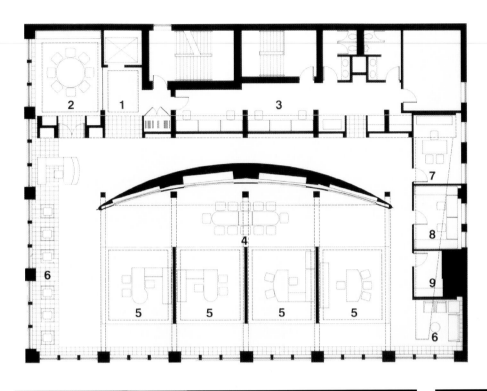

1 Entry
2 Conference
3 Sales area
4 Presentation/resource area
5 Casegood display
6 Seating display
7 Manager's office
8 Technical office
9 Pantry

Top: Floor plan

Left: Sliding doors in cabinetry provide dynamic options

Above: Entry into showroom with identity and company timeline

VOA Associates Incorporated

Suite 1400
224 South Michigan Avenue
Chicago, Illinois, 60604
USA
Telephone: +1 312 554 1400
Facsimile: +1 312 554 1412
Email: info@voa.com

VOA Associates Incorporated, founded in 1969, is a Chicago-based organization with offices in Orlando, Washington, D.C., Columbus, Arlington, and São Paulo, Brazil. The firm offers comprehensive services embracing facility programming, strategic planning, architecture, landscape, and interior design.

VOA establishes close working relationships with each client, which result in numerous innovative design and planning solutions. The firm develops humanistic not mechanistic working environments, allowing for growth and change. VOA strives for enduring design quality that is enhanced over time. Its many repeat clients are testament to this philosophy.

VOA's diversified practice includes financial institutions, investment firms, law firms, educational facilities, master plans, corporate headquarters and offices, hotels and hospitality-related projects, institutional and healthcare facilities, and municipal and transportation related structures. This broad selection of projects allows for a cross-fertilization of ideas and resources as part of VOA's commitment to a superior level of client service. The firm's many awards are attributed to this philosophy.

Huntsman
San Francisco, California, USA
Huntsman Architectural Group

When Huntsman required larger offices, the firm selected a single 20,000-square-foot floor in a downtown San Francisco high-rise. The open plan facilitates circulation between private and public functions and provides an opportunity for the firm to showcase its sustainable design expertise and its penchant for hospitality. Located directly off the elevator lobby, the reception area invites clients and visitors first to a seating area, then to several conference rooms, then to a guest lounge and library.

The main conference room accommodates the entire firm for staff meetings and smaller community events. The adjacent lounge serves as a breakout space for small meetings as well as a reading room for the nearby library. When occupants need privacy, the walnut screen pivots to close off the space. Next to the lounge is a resource and research library that highlights product and design materials. The library is also used for presentations from manufacturer representatives, material selection, as a project room, and for in-house and industry-related seminars.

Beyond the library, meeting rooms and principal offices anchor the open production area, where natural daylight filters through frameless glass walls. The workstations demonstrate the newest technology in flexible workspace and in 'dimmable' fluorescent lighting, serving as examples for clients during tours through the space. The fabric panels from the workstations can be removed easily to change the color palette. In the kitchen, a custom butcher block of laminated plywood becomes the social center of the office every Friday afternoon, when snacks and drinks are served. The wood detail is repeated through the office in various ways, such as in the reception desk and flat files.

Below left: Reception and lobby

Below: Kitchen island

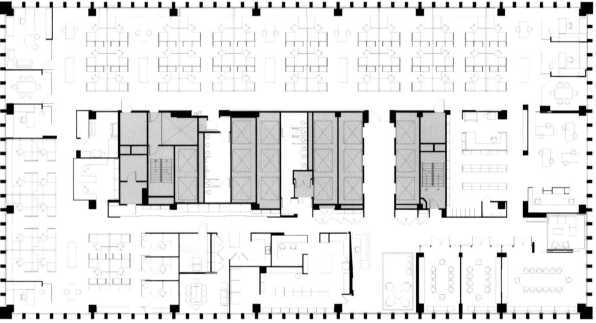

Top left: Main conference room

Top right: Lounge space adjacent to main conference room

Above: Floor plan

Left: Private offices and project rooms

Left: Lounge space with conference rooms in background

Below: Library

Photography: David Wakely Photography

Huntsman Architectural Group

50 California Street, Seventh Floor
San Francisco, California, 94111
USA
Tel: +1 415 394 1212
Fax: +1 415 394 1222
Email: info@huntsmanag.com

Huntsman Architectural Group was founded by architect Daniel Huntsman in 1981 to meet the growing design needs of the San Francisco Bay Area's business community. The firm has been successfully involved in the programming, planning, and project documentation of over 20 million square feet of office space across the United States and internationally.

Huntsman provides a wide range of services to clients including programming, interior design, space planning, building analysis, space utilization studies, architectural design, construction documentation and administration services, as well as all of the conventional adjunct services such as furniture selection and specification, move coordination, cost estimating and project management. Additional consultation services include the production of due diligence and feasibility studies, leasing studies, infrastructure studies, code analysis and review, surveys and reports.

As a full service design firm, Huntsman Architectural Group also has experience in a broad array of project types. Diversity enables the team to efficiently move through multifaceted projects with a clear vision of the project scope and budget.

Iwin

Westwood, Los Angeles, California, USA

Shubin + Donaldson Architects

Iwin wanted a new office space to reflect its active and successful website. The design team was asked to build a flexible work space to accommodate a young staff of engineers, programmers, marketers, and executives that expands and contracts periodically depending on work load. The client wanted the offices to reflect its online presence.

The brief was for a loft-like, industrial, and large open space despite the office-tower setting. To create this atmosphere within a challenging floor plan, the enclosed spaces—such as conference rooms, storage, kitchen, massage room—are attached entirely to the already existing solid walled core in the middle of the space. This allows for open space around the perimeter, while maximizing natural light. Brightly colored Plexiglas panels accent the industrial building materials chosen to give the space a sense of fun and modernism. An interior stairway, with walls of yellow, orange, white, and clear acrylic sheeting, functions as an informal gathering space as well as needed circulation.

Workstations are custom designed of aluminum sheeting with bright-green rolling file standards. A power strut grid in the ceiling with hanging flexible power channels allows the stations to be reconfigured according to need. Conference room and corridor walls are faced with white marker-board.

By using intense lime green—Iwin's corporate color—in combination with other bright tones in a play of transparency and opacity, the architects successfully mirror the client's visual website presence.

Right: Flexible power channels hang from the ceiling grid to support intense computer work

Above: Minimal furnishings and planning are bolstered by bright green—corporate color

Right: Conference rooms are glass enclosed for feeling of openness and transparency

Opposite: Super graphics of company's logo create sense of place in colorful stairwell

Above: Sleek and playful contemporary furniture in black and white is given colorful background

Photography: Tom Bonner

Shubin + Donaldson Architects

3834 Willat Avenue
Culver City, California, 90232
USA
Tel: +1 310 204 0688
Fax: +1 310 204 0219
Email: rshubin@sandarc.com

Shubin + Donaldson Architects, established in 1990 in Culver City, California, is an inventive firm whose current work includes a diverse listing of commercial and residential projects ranging from entertainment-business studios, creative offices and retail stores, to community centers and custom residences. Russell Shubin, AIA, and Robin Donaldson, AIA, have distinguished principals of the 'branded environment,' which they apply to their clients in technology, advertising, Internet, and creative production. Their approach addresses the characteristics of branding, function, adaptability, and anti-hierarchical structures, which are designed with clear interior concepts and commitment to good design as a means to achieve business goals. Their residential work is context and client driven and exudes contemporary living.

Kone Building
Espoo, Finland

SARC Architects

The Kone Building is located on the Finnish coast in Espoo, near Helsinki. A basic block-like shape was chosen for the 18-story tower block. All protruding structures, such as ventilation and the façades' maintenance systems were placed under eaves. Within the building's basic volume, 'breathing spaces' have been created in the form of a two-story entrance vestibule and a glass-walled outdoor terrace located on the 16th floor.

On the building's east and west façades natural light is supplied to the offices through a 7.5-foot-tall strip window. These façades also have an outer secondary glazed façade with silk-screened laminated glass, which prevents excessive heat from penetrating the office spaces. The double façade's 'waterproof coat' also guarantees maximum durability against increased wind and water pressure, which may be experienced higher up in the building.

South-facing panoramic elevators run along an elevator shaft extending the full height of the building. This elevator shaft also acts as a heat valve for the building's offices, controlling heat gain from the glazed south façade. The base and top of the elevator shaft have automatic ventilation hatches through which excess heat can be dispersed. In designing the façade, visible diagonal bracing has been avoided, so that no motifs compete against either the horizontal landscape or the vertical elevator design theme.

The main materials used for the building are glass and steel with Finnish timber used in various forms in the interior. These materials were chosen for their technical durability and their timeless, classic nature.

Left: Elevator lobby

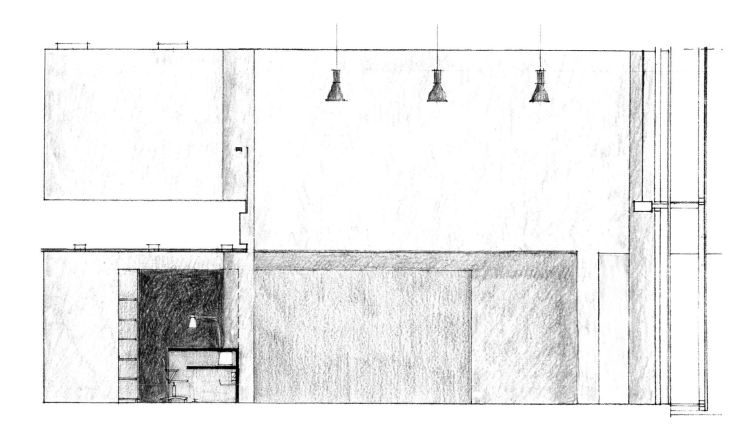

Above: West-east section
Drawing: K&Y Wiherheimo
Below: Entrance lobby

Kone Building

Above: Entrance lobby

Left: Meeting room along south façade

Above: Office floor interior
Photography: Jussi Tiainen

SARC Architects
Vironkatu 3D 00170
Helsinki
Finland
Telephone: +358 9 622 6180
Facsimile: +358 9 6226 1840
Email: sarc@sarc.fi

Originally established in 1965 as Jan Söderlund & Co, the firm was renamed SARC Architects Ltd. in 1998. The managing partners are Professor Antti-Matti Siikala (born 1964) and architect Sarlotta Narjus (born 1966).

The office's commissions are wide ranging including public buildings, offices, housing, renovation, and large-scale planning and development schemes. Several of the practice's projects are prize-winning competition entries, and the office continues to participate in competitions in Finland and overseas.

The firm employs a staff of 25, mostly architects and students of architecture.

March First (formerly USWeb/CKS)
San Francisco, California, USA
IA Interior Architects

To house the 400 people working at its headquarters, March First moved into a four-story 75,000-square-foot former loft-style warehouse in San Francisco's 'Multimedia Gulch' district. The client requested a design that would complement the high-tech edginess of their business and the architecture within the new neighborhood.

Having survived several earthquakes since its construction in 1910, the timber-frame and brick constructed warehouse had a floor slope differential of 36 inches. Several innovative design solutions were incorporated to compensate for the uneven floor with minimal disturbance to the building's historic integrity.

The interior space includes a combination of open and closed offices, a multipurpose room, multiple teaming areas and conference rooms, and a luminous reception desk. An art gallery runs down one office corridor on the first floor. Of the original construction, a brick shear wall remains, running through the middle of the space and original timber columns are positioned equally throughout.

For a modern look, IA incorporated industrial materials such as wire mesh and aircraft cables to provide a suspended canopy over the closed office doorways. IA worked with the engineers to design an elegantly exposed mechanical system and to provide acoustic solutions to muffle the sounds of the building's heat pumps. Bright accent colors were chosen for selected walls, industrial light fixtures, and furniture. Flooring materials range from recycled rubber, to cork and wood planking.

Left: Teaming areas with view of downtown San Francisco

Above: View from
reception through Kalwal
conference room

Top: View into conference room

Middle: Typical office

Left: Conference room with brick shear wall running through

IA Interior Architects

350 California Street, Suite 1500
San Francisco, CA 94104
USA
Telephone: +1 415 434 3305
Facsimile: +1 415 434 0330
Email: k.vanert@interiorarchitects.com

IA Interior Architects is the only global architectural firm to concentrate exclusively on interior architecture. The firm's focus on interiors drove the creation of the company and continues to be its driving force.

Established in 1984, IA has an 18-year track record of delivering successful office interior design projects to a wide range of clients in the United States and internationally. IA today has offices in 13 American cities, London and Shanghai. Its corporate headquarters are in San Francisco.

When IA was founded, it was decided that its architectural practice would be from the inside out, as interior architects. IA Interior Architects believes it takes a special expertise to design an exceptional interior space. As interior architects the firm's approach to design is exclusively focused on how the aesthetics and organization of a space can reflect brand image, improve efficiency and productivity, reduce churn and increase employee satisfaction. A chief goal of the firm is to support its clients' business objectives by enhancing the design and performance of their work environments.

Milano Graduate School

New York, New York, USA

Fox & Fowle Architects, PC

Fox & Fowle was commissioned by New School University to create a home for the Milano Graduate School at 72 Fifth Avenue. The school was formerly housed at a number of locations on the New School campus and this relocation allows the school, for the first time in its history, to have a distinctive campus location and presence.

The building is an early-1900s loft building with exposures and entrances on Fifth Avenue and Thirteenth Street. While the bottom two floors continue to be used by the existing tenant, the Milano School occupies the rest of the building. The building entrances will identify the university and the school as the primary tenants.

While the facility primarily houses offices and workplaces for the faculty and staff, it also features student services floors and both structured and unstructured meeting areas. The building lobbies, elevators, stairwells, windows, and bathrooms have also been renovated.

The Milano School written program stresses that the new facilities should increase communication and collaboration across departments and have a 'professional look…with an edge that…reflects Milano's unique and nontraditional position among policy and management schools.' To this end, Fox & Fowle developed a design that features glass and other translucent materials, maximized open space with exposure to the Fifth Avenue windows, and informal meeting areas and natural gathering spaces. Interior spaces are planned around flexible modules to allow for ease of growth and change.

Left: Translucent panels bring light into interior spaces

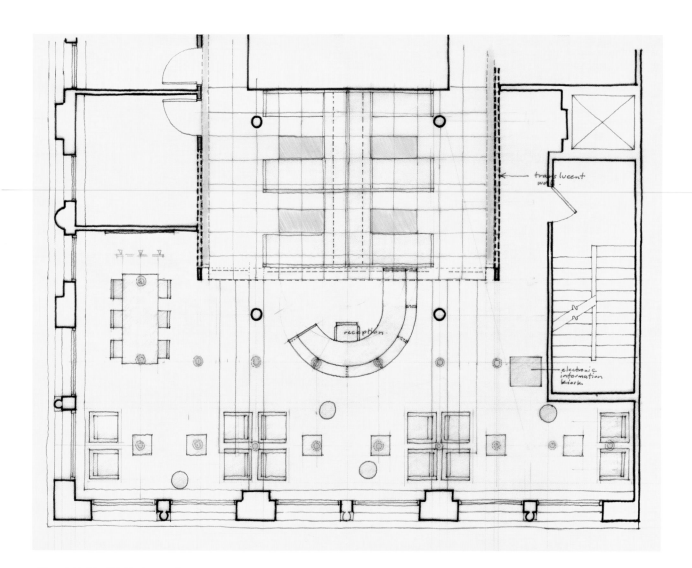

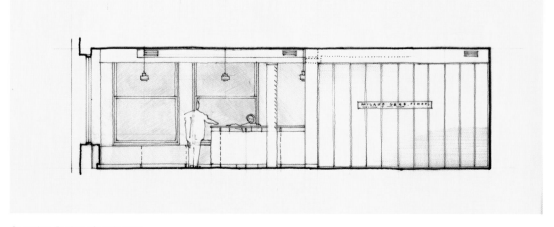

Opposite: Design of perimeter
offices takes advantage of
building's existing
architectural features

Top: Plan of reception area

Above: Interior elevation of
reception area

Fox & Fowle Architects, PC

22 West 19th Street
New York, New York, 10011
USA
Tel: +1 212 627 1700
Fax: +1 212 463 8716
Email: ksibilia@foxfowle.com

Fox & Fowle Architects, P.C. is a 25-year-old architectural, interior design, planning, and urban design firm with a single office located in New York City. The firm has been consistently recognized through local, national, and international design excellence awards and feature articles in the most prestigious design publications. The practice encompasses corporate, civic, cultural, educational, transportation, residential, hospitality, office, retail, and mixed-use projects on a variety of scales.

Fox & Fowle Architects strives to enrich the built environment and provide opportunities for enhanced human experience by engaging in an energetic and diverse dialogue with its changing society. The basis of the work is a collective, rigorous exploration of fit and form, driven by ideas about function, place, the form-making process, and the role of design in human settlement. By taking a truly holistic approach, the result is architecture and planning projects with social, environmental, and aesthetic integrity.

Mindfield Post Production

Marina Del Rey, California, USA

Shubin + Donaldson Architects

Mindfield called for an open plan with six editing bays, reception area, kitchen, and gathering spaces. The post-production facility occupies a warehouse adjacent to the Ground Zero headquarters in Marina del Rey. The architects, who designed the agency's current headquarters, were called back to design this new 20,000-square-foot expansion.

Mindfield's post-production facility is an adjunct to the award-winning design for Ground Zero Advertising, effectively doubling the size of the agency's headquarters. The two buildings are separated by the alley between them, but are connected in design detail. Selected design elements from Ground Zero's headquarters—such as the prefab trusses—have been intentionally included in Mindfield for conceptual consistency. A rhythmic repetition of tightly spaced metal trusses forms the dramatic circulation spine that travels the entire length of the building (240 linear feet).

The basic open-plan work space is continually intersected by arced aluminum-clad walls that weave in and throughout the floor plan. These bold architectural statements result in a series of abstract and dynamically shaped volumes that are used as meeting rooms, editing bays, display nooks, a kitchen, and passageways. The six editing bays are given further design definition with walls surfaced in cold-rolled steel sheets that will be allowed to age to their natural patina. Materials converge as steel meets aluminum in the architectural details of the editing bays.

The project addresses the street with a dramatic entry resulting from the play of walls and volumes. The main conference room is defined by an arced wall that extends through to the exterior and forms the entry vestibule.

Left: Trapezoidal volumes contain editing facilities

Right: Industrial
workstations were
designed by architects

Below: Floor plan shows
arced walls transecting
the space

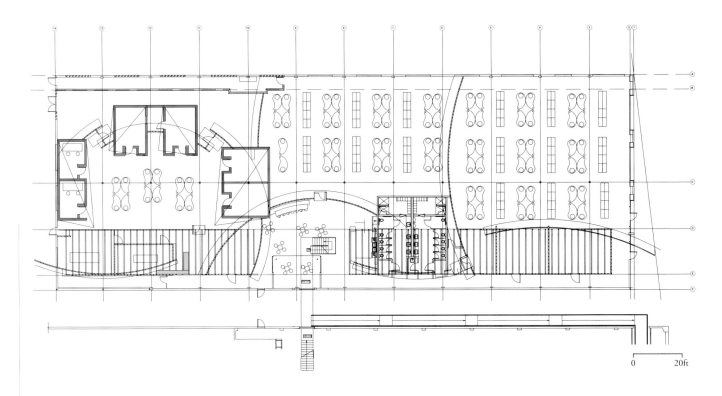

Left: Off-the-shelf trusses define rooms

Below: Reception area adds wood detail to concrete, aluminum, and steel

Bottom: Conference area faces indoor/outdoor space

Above: Curving and arced
walls create idiosyncratic
spaces

Photography: Tom Bonner

Shubin + Donaldson Architects

3834 Willat Avenue
Culver City, California, 90232
USA
Tel: +1 310 204 0688
Fax: +1 310 204 0219
Email: rshubin@sandarc.com

Shubin + Donaldson Architects, established in 1990 in Culver City, California, is an inventive firm whose current work includes a diverse listing of commercial and residential projects ranging from entertainment-business studios, creative offices and retail stores, to community centers and custom residences. Russell Shubin, AIA, and Robin Donaldson, AIA, have distinguished principals of the 'branded environment,' which they apply to their clients in technology,

advertising, Internet, and creative production. Their approach addresses the characteristics of branding, function, adaptability, and anti-hierarchical structures, which are designed with clear interior concepts and commitment to good design as a means to achieve business goals. Their residential work is context and client driven and exudes contemporary living.

New Chancellery Building—Bundeskanzleramt
Berlin, Germany

Axel Schultes Architects

The Chancellery forms part of a chain of federal institutions, 'ribbon' in form and 'thread' by function, adopted as a framework plan for redevelopment following an international competition in 1993. The linchpin of this urban design is called the Civic Forum and, though not yet implemented, it lies at the heart of the Inner Spreebogen (an open space in the Government quarter). The Forum is intended to create a spatial and politico-programmatic link between the large-scale buildings isolated to each side of it.

The Chancellery fulfils its program by means of two five-story, 56-foot-high office tracts between the Forum and the River Spree. The comb-like structure, arranged around winter gardens for easy internal communication and lavish daylighting, accommodates 450 staff. In a 'free program' of political architecture, the executive building was floated into the 180-foot-wide swathe of courtyard and garden which separates the two 60-foot-wide winter garden footprints.

Below: Sky lobby, Chancellor's level
Photography: Werner Hutmacher

Above: Foyer stairs

Photography: Stefan Müller

Top: Foyer under the
Great Wave

Photography: Werner Hutmacher

Above: Chancellor's office

Photography: Stefan Müller

Above: Office format with
double door
Photography: Stefan Müller

Axel Schultes Architects

Lützowplatz 7
10785 Berlin
Germany
Telephone: +49 30 230 888-0
Facsimile: +49 30 230 88888
Email: asa@shultes-architekten.de

Located in Berlin, Axel Schultes founded his own office in 1992 together with longstanding colleagues Charlotte Frank and Christoph Witt. Axel Schultes Architects is a full-service firm working on projects primarily in Germany. Projects include public and urban design, museums, and institutional and commercial buildings.

The practice's interest centers on a firm belief that the quest for spatial articulation is the quintessence of any urban and achitectural enterprise.

Among its most characteristic projects are the Museum of Modern Art in Bonn (1992), and the Crematorium(1998) and the Chancellery (2001), both in Berlin. Competition entries, such as the German History Museum (1988), the Alexandria Libary (1989), the Spreebogen Masterplan (1993) and the Grand Egyptian Museum in Giza (2002) represent in a clear-cut manner Axel Schultes Architects' architectural philosophy.

Norddeutsche Landesbank

Hanover, Germany

Behnisch, Behnisch & Partner

The Norddeutsche Landesbank (Nord LB) needed a publicly accessible administrative building in an intermediate or transitional zone of Hanover, between the city center and a residential district. The 180-foot building is sited on the exterior perimeter block. This high-rise part of the complex detaches itself from the formal order of the city blocks addressing the street, and establishes relationships with a wider context.

The building's central tower is a spiraling superstructure built from masses set at provocative angles. The angles leave various corners cantilevered, a motif continued in other great multi-leveled masses that appear throughout the visually open composition. The tower overlooks a courtyard tucked away inside the building's six-sided exterior. Below the tower, an enormous triangular slab balcony is set on high posts. The courtyard is treated as a landscape, with large-scale water elements and plantings establishing further connections to the surroundings.

The reduction of energy consumption and of carbon-dioxide emissions by utilizing natural resources was one of the major objectives of the building design. Priority was given to window ventilation as the most important source of fresh-air supply to all rooms. Thanks to a double-skin façade on the north side of the block edge and partially on the east and west façades, window ventilation is possible even in these noise-exposed areas of the building.

A daylight redirection system integrated in the external sun-shading system contributes to reducing artificial lighting, allowing the use of direct sunlight without glare problems. State-of-the-art low-pollutant base-load electricity and heat supply by a fuel cell that also serves as a stand-by unit is another detail of the building's energy concept. However, the equipment available today is still rather maintenance intensive.

Left: Art program includes colorful, abstract interpretation of name 'Nord LB'

Right: Internal stairways on office floors foster communication

Below: Employee café reflects dynamism of building's exterior

Bottom: With internal walls and doors of glass, light goes deep into floor plate

Left: Large, food-themed murals give café color and definition

Below: Long red banquettes afford employees views of inner courtyard

Above: New offices
consolidate employees
from 16 offices

Photography: Christian Kandzia

Behnisch, Behnisch & Partner

Los Angeles Office
1517 Park Row
Venice, California, 90291
USA
Tel: +1 310 399 9003
Fax: +1 310 399 9677
E-mail: bbpla@behnisch.com

Behnisch, Behnisch & Partner (founded in 1989) is an internationally renowned full-service practice with a long and distinguished history, working under the leadership of Stefan Behnisch and (since 1997) Günther Schaller in Stuttgart, and Christof Jantzen, associate AIA, in the Los Angeles office. The firm works in both the public and private sectors and has an excellent record in architectural competitions, where the majority of its commissions are gained.

Projects currently under construction or in planning include the Genzyme Building in Cambridge, Massachusetts; the Centre for Cellular and Biomolecular Research in Toronto; Sports Campus Ireland in Dublin; and a school for children with disabilities in Herbrechtingen, Germany. Completed projects include, among others, the Institute for Forestry and Nature Research in Wageningen, The Netherlands; the Museum of Fantasy for the art collector and author Lothar-Günther Buchheim in Bernried (Starnberger See), Germany; the St. Benno School in Dresden, Germany; and the North German State Clearing Bank Building (Nord LB) in Hanover, Germany.

Offitbank
San Francisco, California, USA

IA Interior Architects

When this private financial management company asked IA to design a west coast office for them, three goals were identified. The reception area needed to clearly display its prime California Street location in the heart of San Francisco's financial district. The portion of the plan comprising the private offices and administrative support was required to be efficient and functional, while the portion called the customer area—consisting of reception, main conference room, and two small meeting rooms—should reflect an image of financial success without being ostentatious or excessive. A subtle level of Asian influence in the design was required as an expression of its Pacific Rim location.

The reception area is defined as a circular pavilion by curved metal and translucent glass walls, and a circular architectural geometry composed of an indirect light cove and a floor pattern of granite. The granite is expressed in flamed, honed, and polished surface textures. The main conference room features a custom millwork wall that contains a flat screen monitor and equipment for video conferencing. As in the reception pavilion, lighting is provided through a combination of direct and indirect sources. This lighting theme continues through the private office and administrative support areas via a combination of sculptural light fixtures and discreetly placed downlights. Along the private office fronts, additional ceiling height was carved out of drywall, by strategically routing ductwork above the ceiling. Discreet gestures of Asian imagery are suggested through the use of sliding translucent door panels and the juxtaposition of carefully placed tansu chests.

Left: View from sitting room through reception

Left: Private office detail

Above: Corridor at private offices and open work stations

Below: Conference room sketch

Opposite: Conference room detail

Above: Administrative support in front of private offices
Photography: David Wakeley Photography

IA Interior Architects
350 California Street, Suite 1500
San Francisco, California, 94104
USA
Tel: +1 415.434.3305
Fax: +1 415.434.0330
Email: k.vanert@interiorarchitects.com

IA Interior Architects is the only global architectural firm to concentrate exclusively on interior architecture. The firm's focus on interiors drove the creation of the company and continues to be its driving force.

Established in 1984, IA has an 18-year track record of delivering successful office interior design projects to a wide range of clients in the United States and internationally. IA today has offices in 13 American cities, London and Shanghai. Its corporate headquarters are in San Francisco.

When IA was founded, it was decided that its architectural practice would be from the inside out, as interior architects. IA Interior Architects believes it takes a special expertise to design an exceptional interior space. As interior architects the firm's approach to design is exclusively focused on how the aesthetics and organization of a space can reflect brand image, improve efficiency and productivity, reduce churn and increase employee satisfaction. A chief goal of the firm is to support its clients' business objectives by enhancing the design and performance of their work environments.

Paul-Loebe Building
Berlin, Germany

Stephan Braunfels Architects

The Paul-Loebe Building forms the eastern continuation of the 'Band des Bundes' or Federal Strip in Berlin, a powerful urban plan designed by Axel Schultes, beginning at the Chancellery in the city's west. Situated north of the Reichstag, the Paul-Loebe Building is a committee and office building for members of the German Parliament.

The building's interior is dominated by an atrium-style main hall, which follows the layout of the Federal Strip from west to east. Five office wings are situated to the north and south of the main hall in a comb-like structure. All of the building's internal circulation starts and ends with the main 'atrium' hall. This area is an orientation point for circulation, a meeting place, and a space for holding formal parliament functions. Open galleries connect the hall's component parts horizontally on each level while glazed elevators provide vertical transport to each level.

Skylights in the exposed concrete ceiling grid, the transparent connection solution between the office wings, and cylindrical towers fill the hall with natural light and provide outside views. As a metaphor of democracy, the structure and the transparency of the Paul-Lobe Building ensure unobstructed sightlines and exciting visual connections inside the building.

A light-gray exposed concrete finish was chosen for all structural elements such as the walls and columns. Further finishing detail was executed in glass, coated metal, stained Canadian maple and a grayish-green stone for flooring. This strictly limited canon of surface materials gives the building a very sculptural and monolithic appearance, while also integrating the building's interior space into its urban surroundings.

Left: Top floor beneath main hall roof

Photography: Linus Lintner

Paul-Loebe Building

Opposite: Corridor along main hall crossing one cylinder
Photography: Linus Lintner

Left: Eastern end of main hall with 'Heaven's ladder'
Photography: Ulrich Schwarz

Below: Glass elevator
Photography: Ulrich Schwarz

Bottom: Plan of entrance level

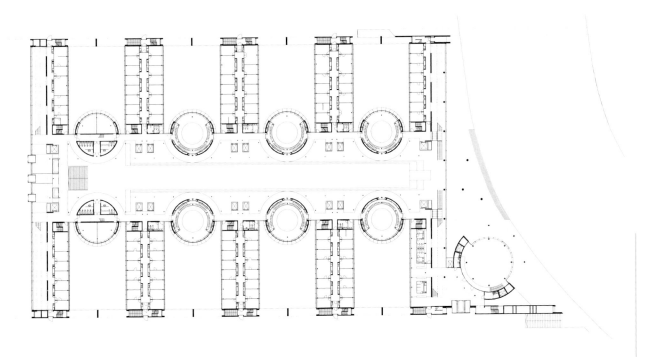

Stephan Braunfels Architects
Kochstrasse 60
10969 Berlin
Germany
Telephone: +49 30 253 7600
Facsimile: +49 30 2537 6050
Email: sba-berlin@braunfels-architekten.de

Stephan Braunfels was born in 1950 and completed his architectural studies at the Technical University of Munich in 1975. In 1978 he established his own firm, Stephan Braunfels Architects, in Munich.

The office regularly enters architectural competitions in both Germany and more broadly, with projects including the Museum for Art and Design in Ingolstadt, the Post Tower in Bonn, and the Science and Technical Museum in Cairo, Egypt. Major projects completed to date include the Pinakothek Modern in Munich, the Paul-Loebe Building for the German federal government in Berlin and a redevelopment/redesign of the Wilhelmshoehe Museum Palace in Kassel.

In 1996, Stephan Braunfels Architects opened its second office in Berlin.

Quartier 30
Berlin, Germany
Atelier Tesar

Quartier 30 is a collaboration between Heinz Tesar, Jo Coenen, and Claude Vasconi. The project began in 1997 as a speculation on the development possibilities of an in-fill block in the established urban fabric of Berlin's Gendarmenmarkt district.

Apart from the building's narrow end façades, the development is seemingly robbed of an urban street-front presence. However, the site's disadvantage revealed an option not usually available to commercial development—the creation of an internal courtyard space located between the new development and the firewall of the neighboring property.

Tesar's design makes the firewall a feature in its own right, incorporating it into a U-shaped courtyard/atrium space. The courtyard/atrium lacks the customary glass roof, instead a solid barrel-vaulted roof terminates the vertical space, with perforations admitting light to the interior. The firewall is finished in high-gloss white to maximize light refraction and illumination of the space.

The courtyard/atrium's gallery levels are constructed from fair-faced concrete, timber, and glass. A row of benches adds to the courtyard's landscape and juxtaposes with the firewall's expanse and the height of the space.

Left: Upper floor view

Right: Interior hall, ground floor with bench

Photography: Christian Richters

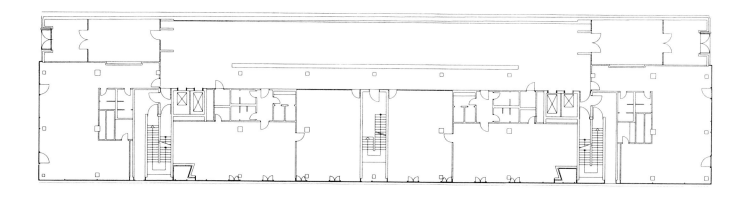

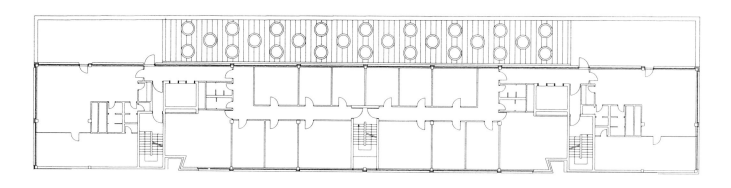

Opposite: Interior hall, ground floor
Photography: Christian Richters

Above: Concept sketch

Left: Water color, Heinz Tesar's sketch of interior hall
Photography: Felix Leutner

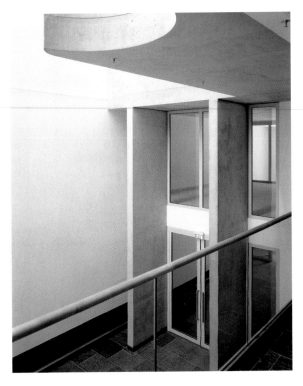

Above: Interior hall, entrance
from above

Right: Interior hall, ceiling view
Photography: Christian Richters

Atelier Tesar

Esteplatz 6/7
A-1030 Vienna
Austria
Telephone: +43 1 715 4898
Facsimile: +43 1 715 4899
Email: atelier.tesar@eunet.at

Heinz Tesar was born in Innsbruck, Austria, in 1939. He studied architecture at the Akademie der Bildenden Künste in Vienna, and opened his own studio in Vienna in 1973 and an office in Berlin in 2000.

In 2000, he received the international Tessenow prize for his life's work to date. He was honoured as, 'an unusual architect, who gave European architecture new impulses with his work. An architect, who defines his position between the late functionalists and postmodernists, coupled with artistic independence and totally rooted in the present, but removed from stylistic trends and short-lived customs.'

Apart from running his own practice, Tesar has taught at Cornell University and Harvard University in the USA, at the ETH in Zurich, and the IUAV in Venice. Currently, he is a visiting lecturer at the Accademia di architettura, Mendrisio, Switzerland.

Storey Hall
Melbourne, Australia
ARM Ashton Raggatt McDougall

The Royal Melbourne Institute of Technology's (RMIT) Storey Hall was commissioned in 1992 with the explicit design aim to create a building that could express RMIT's goal of being at the 'forefront of technical and professional education and real world research.'

The AU$10.5-million project incorporates the historic Storey Hall with a basement student gallery and study area, a two-level art and exhibition gallery, and a 750-seat auditorium. A new six-story annex building adjoins, providing a foyer, services, a kitchen, a basement cinema/theater, storage and five conference rooms on the top floor. High-level audiovisual facilities are incorporated throughout, including a cinema-standard sound system and capability for all modes of projection up to Panavision.

The green theme throughout acknowledges the building's Irish roots (Storey Hall was originally built by the Hibernian Irish Catholic Society in 1887). Green, white, and purple represent the Women's Political Association, a radical feminist organization that occupied the building in 1916.

Penrose tiles adorn the front façade and interior of Storey Hall, invented by world-renowned mathematician Professor Roger Penrose. His 'fat and skinny' tiles reduce the number required for the non-periodic covering of a continuous surface from 20,426 types to just two, as well as engaging in some 'child's play' in non-recursive mathematics, quasi-crystals, fivefold symmetry, 'intelligent grouping,' super-position, 'alternative arrangements,' and even brain plasticity.

Completed in 1996, Storey Hall has received six major professional and industry awards, including a National Royal Australian Institute of Architects (RAIA) Award for Interiors, the RAIA Victorian Architecture Medal for the best building of the year across all categories and the Dulux Color Grand Prix.

Above: View of foyer from balcony

Right: Bay window

ARM Ashton Raggatt McDougall

Level 11, 522 Flinders Lane
Melbourne, Victoria, 3000
Australia
Telephone: +61 3 9629 1222
Facsimile: +61 3 9629 4220
Email: arm.melb@a-r-m.com.au

ARM is a cutting-edge design consultancy with a reputation for innovation, scholarship, and creativity. The practice has long advocated the potential of projects to stand on a world stage as innovative and intelligent. Through creative thought, use of new technology, and hard work, the firm has designed projects to international acclaim.

ARM is Australia's leader in master planning and urban design. The practice's members are keen students of the history of ideas, known for enriching design work by bringing aspects of the precedence to the overall solution. ARM also enjoys a national and international reputation for design excellence publicized in journals, television, books, and postage stamps, receiving in excess of 40 Royal Australian Institute of Architects (RAIA) and industry awards.

The directors and staff are in demand to lecture on design theory and practice, known for their commitment and ability in this fundamental area of architectural endeavor. ARM is also regarded as Australia's leader in computer-generated design, computer imaging and presentation of the 'virtual' building, producing advanced 3D-modeling, animation, video, QuickTime, panoramas and multimedia products.

The Firm

Beverly Hills, California, USA

Shubin + Donaldson Architects

The Firm, a leader in international entertainment and brand management, looked to Shubin + Donaldson Architects to create a new office on Wilshire Boulevard in Beverly Hills. For a client that manages the careers of such varied performers as Korn, Limp Bizkit, the Dixie Chicks, Nick Carter, Vin Diesel, and Mary J. Blige, the architects created a complex space of light, glass, and aluminum.

To mitigate a dark, first-floor former bank space, the architects devised a backlit billboard of glass facing the open work space and defining the private office corridor to fill space with light.

The space is rich in its composition of aged rough concrete columns and a refined aluminum curtain wall system. Translucent layers enhance the 29-foot high open space. The neutral palette of glass, concrete, and aluminum is accented by clear-sealed MDF for workstations and upper-level conference room.

The expansive conference room employs an MDF baffle system with acoustic material behind it. The angled baffle system echoes the plinth-structure of the reception desk, which also houses a monitor for broadcast of The Firm's clients. Bleachers line one wall of the conference room to seat numerous employees during weekly office meetings.

The architect was careful to conceal the ductwork to preserve the purity of the space. The space is a rare combination of industrial materials with fine, precise finishing. Mechanical units had to be inside the space, and run along the ceilings of the offices. The architects created a catwalk for access, which is hidden from view to those on the lower level. The bank vault was converted into a lounge/listening room for The Firm's clients and visitors.

Left: Layers of translucent materials give illusion of natural light

Below: Plinth form of
reception desk is dynamic
shape echoed in upper-
level conference room

Left: Dynamic reception desk maintains urban feeling of concrete and glass

Below: Original bank vault was transformed into lounge

Bottom: The space is rare combination of industrial materials with fine, precise finishing

Above: Stripped columns
and surfaces retain the
urban memory of bank

Photography: Tom Bonner

Shubin + Donaldson Architects

3834 Willat Avenue
Culver City, California, 90232
USA
Tel: +1 310 204 0688
Fax: +1 310 204 0219
Email: rshubin@sandarc.com

Shubin + Donaldson Architects, established in 1990 in Culver City, California, is an inventive firm whose current work includes a diverse listing of commercial and residential projects ranging from entertainment-business studios, creative offices and retail stores, to community centers and custom residences. Russell Shubin, AIA, and Robin Donaldson, AIA, have distinguished principals of the 'branded environment,' which they apply to their clients in technology,

advertising, Internet, and creative production. Their approach addresses the characteristics of branding, function, adaptability, and anti-hierarchical structures, which are designed with clear interior concepts and commitment to good design as a means to achieve business goals. Their residential work is context and client driven and exudes contemporary living.

The HEAR Center

Pasadena, California, USA

Aleks Istanbullu Architects

The HEAR Center, a non-profit community center, was the first facility in the United States to diagnose and treat children with hearing deficiencies.

The client wanted an updated building to foster renewal. The site is a 5000-square-foot, one-story building that was built for The HEAR Center. The reorganization and rehabilitation of the building's interior had to meet specific goals, improve existing circulation inefficiencies, maintain important acoustic characteristics, improve lighting quality and efficiency, and accommodate increased staff.

The design maximizes the sense of spatial flow while simultaneously supporting an increase of indirect lighting. Originally, no windows were provided in the building to maintain acoustical standards. The design introduces skylights at critical locations to provide daylight and accent lighting into the formerly windowless structure.

The space planning was designed to gain additional workstations, which were custom designed by the architect. Other custom cabinetry for the space includes file storage, shelving, reception area desk, and large donor panels. Pastel and natural-color materials are used for surfaces and finishes, adding to the lightness of the space. The finishes and furniture selection provide a soft yet colorful background.

Left: Spatial flow of space maximizes natural light

Above: Skylights were added to formerly windowless space

Above: Minimalist
furnishings accommodate
technical equipment

Right: Millwork was
designed by architect

Left: Subtle colors and light wood create calming atmosphere

Below left: Accent lighting mitigates lack of windows

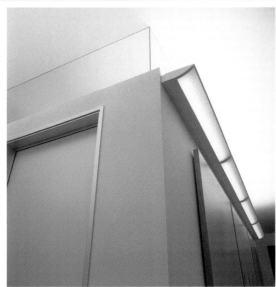

Above: New space was reorganized to create more workstations

Right: Space combines use of natural and artificial light

Photography: Dennis Keeley

Aleks Istanbullu Architects
1659 11th Street, Suite 200
Santa Monica, California, 90404
USA
Tel: +1 310 450 8246
Fax: +1 310 399 1888
Email: aistanbullu@ai-architects.com

Aleks Istanbullu Architects—established in 1986 in Santa Monica—is a creative, highly experienced firm whose work includes the master planning and design of a broad spectrum of public and private projects. Istanbullu's balanced approach to the practice of architecture instils both aesthetic and fiscal responsibility into all projects regardless of size, budget or type. His philosophy of 'strategic design' allows the firm to work in a variety of scales—from corporate to civic and educational, from multi-tenant housing to private residences—to produce an aesthetically refined, feasible, and civically responsible architecture.

Hospitality and Public

Bambu Restaurant

Sydney, Australia

Misho+Associates

The addition of Bambu Restaurant to the recently refurbished Sydney Cove International Passenger Terminal has created an engaging space that pushes many design boundaries. The new fit-out aims to create an intimate atmosphere in an otherwise intimidating industrial space. Misho+Associates' initial concept of an organic sculptural form was realized through close collaboration with artist Horst Kiechle.

The site-specific sculpture's fractal form was achieved by using laminated cardboard panels. The use of this unconventional material on such a large scale within a commercial interior, made it possible to expand on several design and construction possibilities, including fire safety and structural integrity. The sculpture establishes a relationship with the Sydney Opera House through its expressive and organic form, while framing Sydney Cove's spectacular views.

The rigid industrial structure of the existing International Passenger Terminal building has been transformed into an intimate and exciting space. To retain the view through the restaurant, a new cantilevered mezzanine was added to the southern wall. This also posed the challenge of how to accommodate the necessary structure and services within such a tight space. The mezzanine is supported by a large-scale structural steel beam, which echoes the existing industrial nature of the site. The interior's functional areas have deliberately subdued tones and finishes, while strong graphic lines and forms were used to create a more grounded base to complement the fluid sculpture.

Left: View to harbor with moored cruiser

Above: Restaurant with view to The Rocks

Right: Concept sketches

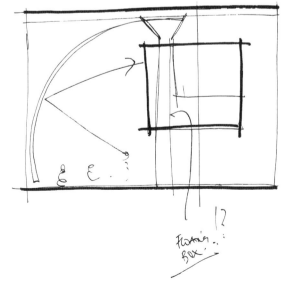

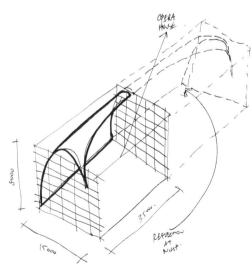

Bambu Restaurant

Above: Mezzanine cocktail lounge

Far left: Interior wave

Left: Interior reflection

Above: View at night
Photography: Simon Kenny

Misho+Associates

PO Box 40
Millers Point, NSW, 2000
Australia
Telephone: +61 2 9247 3555
Facsimile: +61 2 9247 8077
Email: misho@misho.com.au

Misho+Associates is a dynamic young team of passionate architects and interior designers. Located in Sydney, the design studio has a diverse and growing client base. Misho+Associates work across all facets of the industry, ensuring a constantly fresh and enthusiastic approach and an effective solution to each design challenge.

Major projects have included master planning components for key tourism projects such as the Sydney International Airport, and the design and redevelopment of retail and tourism outlets in The Rocks precinct in Sydney.

Challenging design norms in order to achieve functional and aesthetically exciting solutions is a key philosophy for Misho+Associates, as is the belief that interiors, and an individual's experience of a space, must inform the architecture. Among recent commercial projects is the newly completed Bambu Restaurant at Sydney's International Passenger Terminal located opposite the Sydney Opera House.

Bergamot Station Artist Studios

Santa Monica, USA

Pugh + Scarpa

Bergamot Station is an internationally known art center comprising a series of industrial buildings converted into 45 art galleries, including the Santa Monica Museum of Art.

The project evolved as a carefully considered response to its context: a primary palette of materials was established with regard to the existing industrial materials on the site. Corrugated metal, steel, and glass blend in with the surrounding context, while cold rolled steel and translucent lexan panels create moments of distinction in the details of the building that set it apart and help establish its idiosyncratic identity.

Nestled in between warehouse buildings on a narrow site, the façade facing the interior of the site unfolds itself gracefully along a canted corrugated-metal plane that extends itself into the residual space produced by the adjacent buildings. This residual space is now often used to host outdoor receptions and special events.

The building's interior is simply organized. The ground floor features an open plan that allows maximum flexibility of use and reuse. Simply treated in its finishes and details, the ground-floor interior is conceived as a vessel for program to animate. A separate entrance leads to the three artist loft units above. Each of these maximizes its potential for spaciousness and light, while also creating moments of intimacy and enclosure.

Below left: View of primary living space from sleeping loft

Below right: Detail elevation of fireplace and guest bathroom

Right: Interior stair to loft entry

Below left: View from front entry into large loft

Below right: Living area of smaller lofts

Bottom: Typical section

Opposite: Overall view of large loft. Custom carpet and coffee tables by Pugh + Scarpa

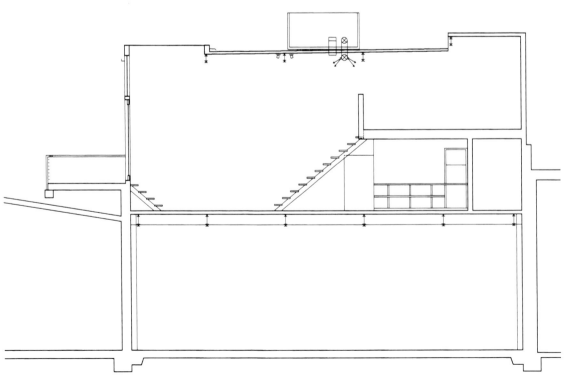

Bergamot Station Artist Studios

Above: View from dining
area looking north

Photography: Marvin Rand

Pugh + Scarpa
2525 Michigan Ave, Suite F1,
Santa Monica, California, 90404
USA
Telephone: +1 310 828 0226
Facsimile: +1 310 453 9606
Email: info@pugh-scarpa.com

Pugh + Scarpa is an architecture, engineering, interior design, and planning firm founded in Santa Monica in 1991. Pugh + Scarpa has grown to a firm of 43 professionals and, currently, is working on an assortment of commissions for public, private, and institutional clients. The firm maintains offices in Santa Monica, California, San Francisco, California, and Charlotte, North Carolina. Gwynne Pugh AIA, Lawrence Scarpa AIA, and Angela Brooks AIA, are the sole principals and the firm is consciously structured to ensure their participation in each project.

Brasserie
New York, New York, USA
Diller + Scofidio

The prospect of redesigning one of New York's legendary restaurants in one of the world's most distinguished modernist buildings was as inviting as it was daunting. The architecture of the new restaurant respectfully challenges many of the tenets of modernism.

After removing all traces of Philip Johnson's interior, the rough concrete surfaces of the original space have been relined with new skins of wood, terrazzo, tile, and glass. These thin 'liners' often lift from their surfaces to become structural, spatial and functional components. For example, the madrone floor peels up while the pear-wood ceiling peels down and is molded into seating as part of a continuous wrapper around the main dining space. Pear-wood skins in the rear dining room peel from the plaster ceiling and wall to become floating partitions, which delaminate into illuminated veneers.

The design emphasizes the social aspects of dining. Entrance from the street is transformed into the ritual of 'making an entrance.' Initially, a sensor in the revolving entry door triggers a video snapshot that is added to a continuously changing display over the bar, announcing every new patron.

Other features include a slender space flanking the dining area that is sliced into private booths by a series of tall, upholstered slabs tipped up on end and propped on steel legs. The men's and women's restrooms are separated physically yet connected visually by semi-transparent honeycomb panels and a cast resin sink spanning both spaces with a single drain. At the bar, tripod-steel supports carry bar seats injected with medical gel.

Below: Pear-wood ceiling peels down as continuous wrapper around main dining space

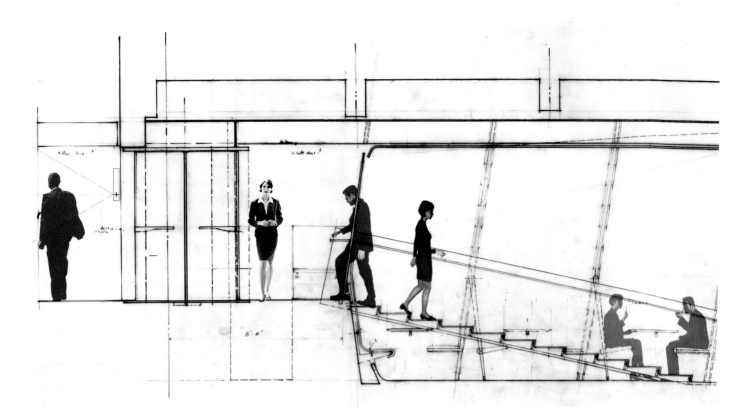

Top: Section

Above: Video snapshots over bar announce new arrivals

Right: Molded seating part of continuous wrapper around main dining space

Top: Entrance from street—makes possible concept of 'making entrance'

Left: Tall upholstered slabs slice between private booths

Above: Entrance stair
Photography: Michael Moran

Diller + Scofidio
36 Cooper Square, Floor 5
New York, New York, 10003
USA
Email: info@dillerscofidio.com

Diller + Scofidio is a collaborative, interdisciplinary studio that fuses architecture, the visual arts, and the performing arts. The team is primarily involved in thematically driven experimental work that takes the form of temporary and permanent site-specific installations, multimedia theater, print and architectural commissions.

Elizabeth Diller and Ricardo Scofidio are the recipients of the MacArthur Foundation Award, the first given in the field of architecture. They have recently been awarded a James Beard Foundation Award for Best New Restaurant for the *Brasserie*.

Elizabeth Diller is Professor of Architecture at Princeton University and Ricardo Scofidio is Professor of Architecture at The Cooper Union. Their bilingual book, *Back to the Front: Tourisms of War/Visite aux Armee: Tourismes de Guerre* was published by the FRAC Basse-Normandie. A book of their work, *Flesh* is in its third reprint by Princeton Architectural Press. Their new book, *Blur: the Making of Nothing* will be published this year by Harry N. Abrams, Inc.

Chosun Galbee Restaurant
Los Angeles, California, USA
Studio RCL

Studio RCL's objective was to design a structure that catered to the lifestyles of both Korean and non-Korean customers. Chosun Galbee Restaurant is a building that combines both traditional and modern elements to appeal to a wide range of tastes and functions, resulting in a unique style that sets it apart from other restaurants in the community. The restaurant also needed to operate efficiently with the seamless incorporation of design, function, and profitability.

The project began as an interior remodel of an existing building but quickly progressed to the construction of a new building, interior design (including original custom furniture), exterior patio space, parking lot, and landscaping. Open lines of communication between the design team and the contractor were essential in keeping the project on track. Flexibility and quick assessments were critical. Every change and development in the project's scope evolved into an opportunity for innovative and functional design solutions.

The architect used the owner's requirement of private dining areas as a guiding influence in the organization of the floor plan. The placement of two bamboo-lined private dining rooms at the south end of the building acts as a buffer between the interior and exterior communal eating areas. The rooms themselves contain partial walls which function as visual screens, restricting views into the space, while the gaps above, below, and between these walls admit light and provide a feeling of openness.

Below: Patio area and view from entryway
Photography: Mark Luthringer

Above: Patio areas and
bamboo-clad private
dining rooms

Right: Entry area with
hostess counter and bar

Photography: Benny Chan

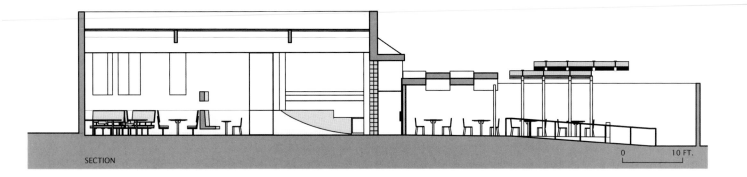

SECTION

0   10 FT.

Top: Section

Left: Main dining area with stainless-steel vents and table barbecues

Above: Private dining room with custom-made aluminum plate chairs

Photography: Mark Luthringer

Above: Entryway and steel trellis
Photography: Mark Luthringer

Studio RCL
1257 Vista Court
Glendale, CA 91205
USA
Telephone: +1 818 242 4268
Facsimile +1 818 242 4168
Email: rcl@rcl.net

Studio RCL was founded in 1990 by Richard Cutts Lundquist, AIA. Since its inception in the Echo Park area of Los Angeles, the firm has designed and built a series of acclaimed residential and commercial projects. These include several well-known clothing stores, a highly popular and successful restaurant in the Koreatown area of Los Angeles and a 50-room Best Western Hotel tower in British Columbia, Canada. Their residential projects range from remodeling to major additions for homes in Santa Monica, Brentwood, Hancock Park, Los Angeles, and Glendale.

Studio RCL's work has been published locally and internationally. It has also been included in various exhibitions such as the American Institute of Architects' 'Residential Architecture' exhibit and the 'New Blood' exhibit at the Pacific Design Center.

Early Childhood Development Center

St Clare's Parish Center, New York, New York, USA

Stephen Perrella Architect

Salvadeo Associates Architects PC (Architect of Record)

The renovation of this building's ground floor was seen as an opportunity to emphasize the importance of relations and relationships as opposed to normal practices that isolate 'entities' in space and time. The design-theme explored ideas including: inside and outside, a youth horizon of 3 feet, 6-inches high versus an adult horizon, the spiritual and the secular, color and form, public and private, space and time, as well as a host of anticipated yet unexpected relations that opens a space up for interpretation.

The art room was a space in which an erasure of all dialectical relations could be explored. By adopting Stephen Perrella's theory called 'Hypersurface,' the architects designed the walls to be multi-functional and specifically shaped, incorporating furniture and other features into them. This tactic makes the walls into space dividers while program objects become open to interpretation, in terms of their use and specific functions.

The overall project scheme configures two diagrams: half of the space, beginning with the lobby, is an articulation of embodied being and materiality in an accelerated Cartesianism. The classrooms delineating the other half of the preschool are organized by a cone-shaped juncture of corridors. Interwoven and apparent throughout the space is a continuous 3-foot-six-inch horizon created specifically for children. This zone provides children with a space that relates directly to their stature and reinforces their presence in the school.

A double-compound curved wall in the main lobby establishes a flow through the space with a slight disjunction from the lobby through the hallway to a cone, registering the 'secular' and 'religious' systems of the space. The lobby ceiling that connects to the 'angel-cone,' is a one-of-a-kind, algorithmically curved, metal ceiling that randomly disperses sound created by a 'parade of youth.'

Left: View toward lobby from art room

Above: View from art
room into exhibit hall
lobby

Right: Art room interior—
this room overlooks
gymnasium

Early Childhood Development Center

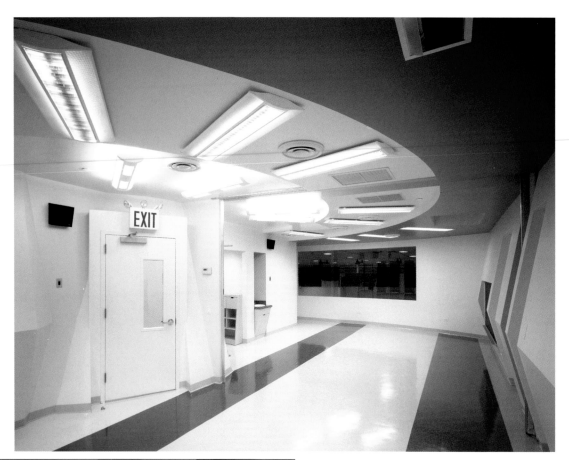

Above: View of classroom that overlooks gymnasium

Left: View from double-zone exhibit gallery toward front lobby

Above: Lobby to preschool
showing deconstructed art
room

Photography: Zbig Jedrus

Stephen Perrella Architect
165 Princeton Ave
Staten Island, New York, 10306
USA
Telephone: +1 718 986 0038
Facsimile: +1 718 979 9296
Email: hypersurface@si.rr.com

Stephen Perrella is an architect who spent 12 years at Columbia University GSAP editing and designing architectural publications with Bernard Tschumi. During that time Perrella developed his theoretical ideas called 'Hypersurface,' which entails negotiating the simultaneous topologization of architectural form with the influx of digital media.

Hypersurface has been the focus of Perrella's past decade of international lectures and seminars, and the St Clare's project is a first step toward applying his theoretical ideas into everyday architecture. Perrella greatly enjoyed his collaboration on the St Clare's project with Architect of Record David Businelli and his enthusiasm for complex ideas.

Ichthus College
Rotterdam, The Netherlands
24H-architects

A proposal was made to renovate one of Ichthus College's departments. This involved redesigning the interior of an entire floor in the former Ned Lloyd building on the Zalmhaven in Rotterdam. The building is a nondescript office complex near the city center. Hemmed in on all sides by office and residential blocks, the 1970s complex, clad in garish panels, is faceless and boring. Therefore, maximum energy was spent on creating an inspiring interior as an antidote to the featureless exterior.

The building envelope enclosed a floor plan comprising a series of bays interrupted by an 'obstacle course' of service cores and columns. College spaces were also organized into an uninspiring 'straightjacket' of luminous walls. In order to reorganize these spaces, the classrooms were separated from the foyer and woven around the maze of columns and cores, so that the existing office shell vanished without trace.

Digital prints depicting colorful natural imagery, blown up almost beyond the point of abstraction, now wrap the tilted, ribbon-like outer walls of the four classroom clusters. Circulation space between clusters expands and contracts, its flow broken by rhythmical vertical panels of translucent glass illuminated from behind. A sculptural 'fish' has been placed in the floor's center—the volume of this structure contains three pouch-like meeting rooms crowned by a star-spangled ceiling, while simultaneously providing a physical separation between the public space and administration offices. In addition, the sculpture's tail tapers off and to form a comfortable bench.

Below: Images are blown up prints featuring small boxes of plants and flowers from fragrance retailer Sephora

Above: 'Sculptural fish' in foyer separating public space and administration offices

Left: Narrow passage leads to pouch-like meeting rooms in 'sculptural fish'

Above: Views of city skyline are printed on fabric skirting perimeter walls

Below: Circulation routes between classrooms. All ducts and pipes have been painted and left exposed. Sanitized perspex panels conceal flouresent tubes

Above: Custom-made tables and chairs in foyer designed by 24H. Upholstered puzzleSIT chairs interlock to form 6-meter-long lounge element

Photography: Christian Richters

24H-architects
Van Nelleweg 1206
3044 BC Rotterdam
The Netherlands
Telephone: +31 10 750 3150
Facsimile: +31 10 750 3160
Email: Info@24h-architecture.com

Since its inception on January 1 2001, 24H-architecture has been involved in various commissions of different scales. The 24H team combines the dynamic of a young office with a decade of top-level architectural experience.

It is the ambition of founders, Maartje Lammers and Boris Zeisser, to create a design company that, over time, will cover the different disciplines required in developing urban or architectonic projects. These disciplines range from feasibility studies to construction coordination and project management. In this ambition, partially lies the strength of the concept for 24H: only intensive involvement in all stages of the project can guarantee a result of outstanding quality.

The design firm's objective is to establish a brand name, 24H, which will denote architecture and products of extreme quality and sensitivity. The need for detail and decoration becomes evermore apparent in current post-20th-century society.

Imperial War Museum – North

Trafford, Manchester, UK

Studio Daniel Libeskind LLC

The Imperial War Museum of the North deals with the conflicts that have shaped the 20th century and those that will continue to influence the future. The building combines culture and regeneration, craft and design, in order to give the public a striking emblem, which illuminates both the traditional and the new.

The building is a constellation composed of three interlocking shards. The Earth Shard forms the generous and flexible museum space. It signifies the exposed, earthly realm of conflict and war. The Air Shard with its projected images, observatory, and education spaces serves as a dramatic entry into the museum. The Water Shard forms the platform for viewing the Manchester Ship Canal, by which the museum is located, with its restaurant, cafe, deck, and performance space.

These three shards together—Earth, Air and Water—represent 20th-century conflicts fought on dramatic terrain, on earth, at sea, and in the skies, by military, naval and air forces.

Below: Earth Shard:
main exhibition space

Above: Main museum stair

Right: Earth Shard: main
exhibition with time line

Left: Museum entrance
lobby

Below: Air Shard: museum
entrance

Above: Water shard:
restaurant
Photography: Len Grant

Studio Daniel Libeskind LLC

2 Rector Street, 9th Floor
New York, New York, 100006
USA
Tel: +1 646 452 6180
Fax: +1 646 452 6198
Email: info@daniel-libeskind.com

Daniel Libeskind is an international figure in architectural practice and urban design. He is well known for introducing a new critical discourse to architecture and for his multidisciplinary approach. His practice extends from building major cultural institutions including museums and concert halls, landscape and urban projects, to stage design, installations, and exhibitions.

INHOLLAND University

Rotterdam, The Netherlands

(EEA) Erick van Egeraat associated architects

The INHOLLAND University is situated at the Kop van Zuid in Rotterdam. The adjacent harbor area houses 19th- and early 20th-century industrial architecture and the university refers to this area's urban scale and typology.

The client's objective was to create a flexible 21st-century building, radiating transparency but fitting into the 19th-century brick building concept of the city's urban plan. The redevelopment also allows for the university to be partially rented out eventually, or to be converted into an office building.

Consisting of two wings enclosing a central atrium space, the project maximizes on the site's available space. Specific functional areas and public spaces are situated on the first three floors with classrooms located on the upper six floors. The heart of the project is the atrium space along the south façade, which develops over the full height of the building.

Materials are predominantly cobalt blue screen-processed glass and clear glass overlooking remarkable views, and creating an expression for the open character of the building, which is also part of the university's trademark.

Left: Atrium space

Top, above and right:
Atrium space along south
façade is building's heart,
which develops over
building's full height

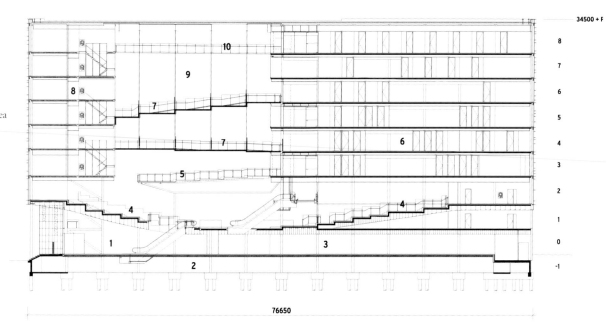

1 Entrance hall
2 Parking garage
3 Shops
4 Stepped floor area
5 Study area
6 Offices and flexible
  work spaces
7 Suspended study area
8 Administration
9 Atrium
10 Suspended bridge

Above: Section

Left: Study area with view over harbor

Above: Connecting bridges in atrium

Left: Transparency and openness are project's main elements

Photography: Christian Richters

(EEA) Erick van Egeraat associated architects

Calandstraat 23
3016 CA Rotterdam
The Netherlands
Telephone: +31 10 436 9686
Facsimile: +31 10 436 9573
Email: eea.nl@eea-architects.com

Erick van Egeraat was born in 1956 in Amsterdam. He graduated with honors from the University of Delft's Architectural Department in 1984. Since 1980, he has worked with Francine Houben, Henk Döll, Chris de Weijer and Roelf Steenhuis, with whom he founded Mecanoo Architects in Delft in 1984. In 1995 he established his own firm in Rotterdam. Currently, (EEA) Erick van Egeraat associated architects has offices in Rotterdam, Budapest, and London, and works with permanent staff of 100 people.

Library, Technical University Delft

Delft, The Netherlands

Mecanoo

The library of the University of Technology (TU) Delft is an unashamedly futuristic, almost inviolable building, which does not tolerate any other construction close to it.

The steel and glass structure's exterior is covered with grass so that it looks more like a landscape than a building. The lawn covering ascends at one corner like a piece of paper to form the library's inclined roof, and this area can also be walked on. From here, a round, tapered and open structure rises up, and this has already been dubbed as 'the cone'. At the foot of the cone, in the central hall, the interior presents a science-fiction-like appearance.

The library's interior is presented in a user-friendly layout and its striking visual design provides an ambience of calm, studiousness, knowledge, inspiration, and ambition for students and visitors. Study spaces are spread throughout hung floors in the central cone with additional study space located along the library's façade.

Below: Central hall with huge cone and four-story-high bookcase hanging in front of deep-blue rear wall

Library, Technical University Delft

Opposite: Supported on
splayed-steel columns,
cone houses four levels of
traditional study spaces
connected by helical stair

Top: Extending forty
meters above grade and
floodlit at night, cone acts
as beacon on campus day
and night

Above: Cone is articulated
by 1500-millimeter-wide
necklace of glazing in
plane of roof

Left: Against Sahara-
colored floor, hard,
metallic ceiling is softened
by light coming from
columns. Columns support,
illuminate and heat
building

Below: Library's great
spaciousness, with its large
central hall, has cathedral-
like effect—imposing but
inviting

Photography: Christian Richters

Mecanoo
Oude Delft 203
2621 DG Delft
The Netherlands
Telephone: +31 15 2798 100
Facsimile: +31 15 2798 111
Email: info@mecanoo.nl

Since building the competition-winning design for social housing for young people on Rotterdam's Kruisplein (1982–1985), the Delft-based office of Mecanoo, founded in 1984, has been working steadily on an extensive and varied oeuvre.

In the early years, work consisted mainly of social-housing projects in urban-renewal areas. In 1987, the firm was awarded the Rotterdam Maaskant prize for Young Architects for the high quality of their work. Today, with a staff of around 55, directed by Francine Houben, work focuses on complex, multifunctional buildings and integral urban developments, combining urban planning, landscaping, architecture, and interior design.

With around 300 projects, over 100 realized and various projects under construction or in preparation, the practice is very successful in the Netherlands and Europe. Mecanoo's work combines concern for the expressive potential of space, form, and material with a reflective practice on dialogue with clients and future users.

Long Island University

Brooklyn, New York, USA

Mitchell/Giurgola Architects, LLP

Long Island University has constructed a new building in the heart of the Brooklyn campus, to satisfy the needs of a rapidly growing student and faculty population. LIU's programmatic requirements for the Pratt Center included new space to relieve cramped and inadequate classrooms, student services, and supporting resources. It also incorporated computer labs and flexible spaces wired for the school's burgeoning technological needs.

The six-story Pratt Center welcomes students and faculty from the main campus walk at its primary entrance, and from the north through the lobby of the Triangle Theater. The most prominent façade of the building is clad in glass, giving relief to the long, windowless backside of the Metcalfe Building.

The lobby runs the length of the site from east to west, anticipating future demolition of an adjacent building and the eventual connection to Flatbush Avenue, allowing a convenient passage to the center of the campus. A tall stone-clad wall defines the public corridor from the departmental office suites and classrooms, flanking it while simultaneously extending beyond the face of the building to mark the entry. Natural light diffuses through the two three-story atria that repeat the corridor/lobby arrangement. The ends of each corridor terminate in a lounge affording views into campus or across Flatbush Avenue.

Below: Fifth-floor lounge
at west end of building

Above right: Looking up atrium

Right: Fifth-floor corridor and atrium

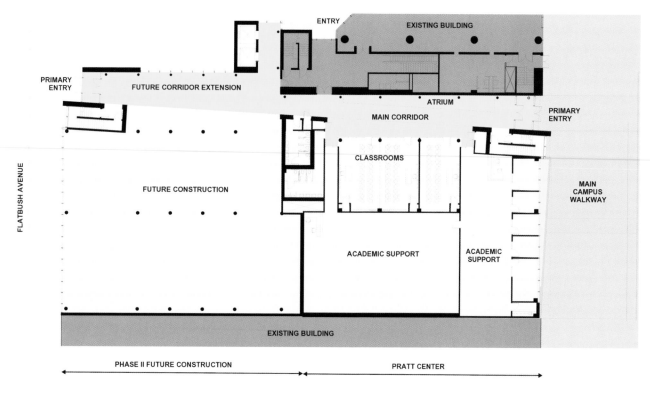

PRIMARY ENTRY

FUTURE CORRIDOR EXTENSION

ENTRY

EXISTING BUILDING

ATRIUM

PRIMARY ENTRY

FLATBUSH AVENUE

MAIN CORRIDOR

FUTURE CONSTRUCTION

CLASSROOMS

MAIN CAMPUS WALKWAY

ACADEMIC SUPPORT

ACADEMIC SUPPORT

EXISTING BUILDING

PHASE II FUTURE CONSTRUCTION

PRATT CENTER

Above: First-floor plan

Right: Study Center and administrative offices

Below: Classroom

Above: East entrance
Photography: Jeff Goldberg/Esto

Mitchell/Giurgola Architects, LLP

170 West 97th Street
New York, New York, 10025
USA
Tel: +1 212 663 4000
Fax: +1 212 866 5006
info@mitchellgiurgola.com

The New York office of Mitchell/Giurgola Architects offers a comprehensive range of architectural services from master planning and urban design, research and programming, new buildings, additions and renovations, to interior and graphic design. The firm is organized as a studio to develop designs for highly complex building programs. Buildings for education are a hallmark of the practice.

Mitchell/Giurgola maintains a distinguished record of creating functional and memorable spaces for cultural, educational, and public uses and has also engaged in numerous large-scale urban design and planning projects. Six partners and a professional staff of thirty-five work with their clients to tailor designs to the clients' specific procedural, programmatic, and architectural needs. Building designs are derived from a direct response to the project program and the context of the site. Mitchell/Giurgola's projects have been recognized with both technical and design awards on the national level, including AIA Honor Awards for Architecture and the prestigious Lab of the Year award from R&D Magazine.

LuLu
San Francisco, California, USA
CCS Architecture

Harmony and chaos in a fire-lit Mediterranean scene—this was the vision behind LuLu, the epic 8000-square-foot restaurant that helped catalyze San Francisco's South of Market neighborhood. LuLu is an integral part of the Yerba Buena cultural district.

CCS transformed a vacant warehouse into a Roman plaza, inspired by Michelangelo's great Piazza del Campidoglio, with its trapezium-shaped plan and centralized ellipse. The architecture seeks a balance of contrasts between the public arena and the individual experience of place. The interplay of figure and ground, people and objects, is expressed through the dramatic composition of the space and the activities it contains.

The existing double-barrel vaulted roof was peeled open at the front and rear to admit sunlight and reveal activity from within. A new front wall bows inward to invite passage and movement. The exhibition kitchen enjoys a prominence similar to that given to the Senatorio building in Michelangelo's composition. From here emerges the fire-roasted food, which fuels the celebration of the sacred and the mundane.

Below: Main dining space with bar beyond

Right: Wood-fired
exhibition kitchen

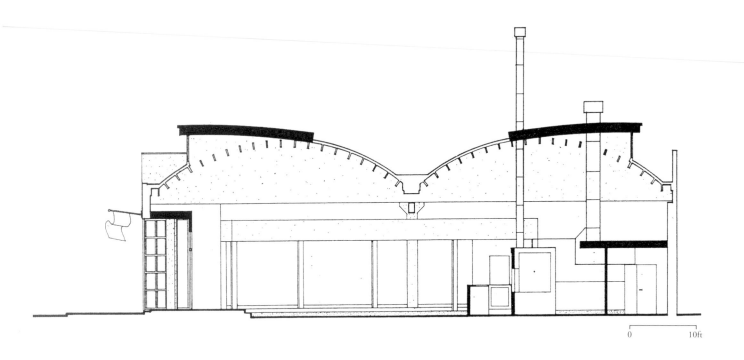

Above: Exterior elevation

Below: Bar

Below right: Side dining space with open kitchen beyond

Above: Façade at dusk

Photography: David Duncan Livingston,
Michael O'Callahan, Bryan Natinsky

CCS Architecture
44 McLea Court
San Francisco, California, 94103
USA
Tel: 415-864-2800
Fax: 415-864-2850
Email: info@ccs-architecture.com

CCS Architecture, the design studio of Cass Calder Smith, is dedicated to excellence in Architecture and Design. Since it's inception in 1990, CCS has designed a diverse range of public and private buildings and interiors for living, working, eating, and more. The firm has gained international acclaim for the architectural and commercial success of restaurant projects, while the uniqueness of residential, commercial, and mixed-use projects has met with an unusual degree of owner satisfaction and media praise.

CCS seeks to explore opportunities of maximum potential and express them at a scale appropriate to each project. The work is firmly based in the modernist idiom where innovation and creativity are balanced by common sense and experience. The firm is known for creating projects with exceptional spatial and material qualities, and for providing outstanding professional service.

Model Arts and Niland Centre
Sligo, Ireland
McCullough Mulvin Architects

Built in 1861, the Model School in Sligo was designed with a long façade to The Mall on a slope over the street. The ground rises behind to form a large walled courtyard on an upper level. Behind the main façade, the rooms were disparately cranked into awkward wings around grim exercise yards on several different levels.

When McCullough Mulvin Architects became involved, the building was being used as an art center. The project brief was to enhance its function to house the town's significant Jack B. Yeats painting collection under optimum environmental conditions, to facilitate international exhibition loans, and to host contemporary visual arts exhibitions. A small performance space was required to cater for music, film and educational spaces, and study facilities. Administration and ancillary spaces for these functions and for festivals run by the organization were also required.

The project offered unique opportunities for intervention, to make a modern gallery and public space attached to the old rooms. Yards were removed to generate a roof-lit central room raised in section over a basement store around which all activities of the building are organized. The Niland Gallery, a rectangular cedar- and zinc-clad box containing gallery space over a café, slides across to the north side to close the new space. A sequence of strongly defined north lights to provide shadow-free diffused daylight for the collection is countered by similar lights turned through 90 degrees to light the atrium.

Contemporary gallery spaces are housed in the carefully redesigned old part of the building. The entrance has been dramatically enlarged inside to create an appropriate arrival and orientation zone. From this oblique view of the atrium and hidden light source, it is possible to see the intent of the circulation, a diagonal route of staircases stepping up a steep hill and mediating between the existing entrance and the new gallery. Environmentally, the new galleries are designed to achieve optimum standards of environmental control without air handling or conditioning.

Above left: West sunlight through atrium roof lights

Above right: Atrium from Niland Gallery entrance

Below: Atrium with steps
to Niland Gallery

Above left: Entrance with view to atrium beyond

Left: Niland Gallery with municipal collection

McCullough Mulvin Architects
2 Leeson Park
Dublin 6
Ireland
Telephone: +353 1 497 2266
Facsimile: +353 1 497 9592
Email: macmul@eircom.net

Based in Dublin, McCullough Mulvin Architects is one of Ireland's most prestigious and awarded young architecture practices. Established in the late 1980s by Valerie Mulvin and Niall McCullough, it now boasts a number of Ireland's best young architects.

The office has worked on major cultural projects like the Abbey Theatre, in the Temple Bar regeneration area (where the practice has also designed the Temple Bar Galleries, Black Church Print Studios, and Music Centre) and in the recently completed Model Arts and Niland Gallery in Sligo. The firm's portfolio features civic office buildings that provide increased standards of public service, like the Dun Laoghaire-Rathdown County Hall to civic offices in Donegal and Sligo, residential designs for houses and apartments, and new libraries such as the Waterford City Library and the joint design for the Ussher Library in Trinity College.

The projects display the practice's interest in modern things. Its architects like to keep an open mind to architecture's projections about how people live and work in Ireland, and the opportunities arising from briefs to form new and unique public spaces that display evolving attitudes to land, history, and memory. Many of the projects are either in sensitive contexts and reflect a specific response to site and place, or are modern interventions into existing buildings, an open-ended exploration of scale, materials, and form.

Morimoto Restaurant

New York, New York, USA

Karim Rashid

Morimoto, the client, only had two requests on commissioning this project. He wanted to be seen when working, as on a stage (as he is a known celebrity), and he requested that nothing in the bathrooms be touched by hand, instead everything should be fully automatic.

The design concept for this project began with the typology of food. It then developed into a long Cartesian grid of booths juxtaposed with a fluid organic space. The bamboo ceiling and floor become one undulating organic envelope that starts out very low in the entrance, symbolic of bowing in traditional Japanese restaurants.

The Cartesian grid of glass walls in the center of the space is made of frosted glass with embedded LEDs spaced every third of an inch. The backs of the booths are made of 6-inch-thick hollow frosted-glass boxes. The boxes of glass and LEDs are recessed in the floor so that light almost appears to glow from the floor below, creating an ephemeral and poetic feeling. The LEDs are programmed to gradually fade from one color to the next over a 15-minute interval creating a change of atmosphere in the restaurant over the course of a meal.

Below: Restaurant from upstairs bar

Photography: David Joseph

Left: Pair seating on side of restaurant
Photography: Karim Rashid

Below: Pair seating with wall sculpture
Photography: Karim Rashid

Bottom: Sculpture and digital art in entrance
Photography: David Joseph

Above: Booths and LED wall dividers
Photography: David Joseph

Left: Booths and LED wall dividers
Photography: David Joseph

Karim Rashid
357 West 17th Street
New York, NY 10011
USA
Telephone: +1 212 929 8657
Facsimile: +1 212 929 0247
Email: office@karimrashid.com

Karim Rashid was born in Cairo, Egypt in 1960. He received a Bachelor of Industrial Design from Carleton University in Ottawa, Canada in 1982. Then he pursued graduate design studies in Naples, Italy, with Ettore Sottsass and others, before moving to Milan for a year to the Rodolfo Bonetto Studio.

On his return to Canada, Rashid worked for seven years with KAN Industrial Designers. While at KAN,

he co-founded and designed the Babel Fashion Collection and North from 1985–91. In 1993 he opened his own practice in New York.

Rashid has worked for numerous clients globally such as Prada, Yahoo!, Issey Miyake, Estée Lauder, Tommy Hilfiger, Giorgio Armani, Sony, Maybelline, and Citibank among others.

Nursery School
Hombroich Island, Neuss, Germany
Oliver Kruse

Located at the westernmost edge of the Hombroich museum island, is the 'Children's Island,' a nursery school designed to accommodate approximately 20 children.

Architect Oliver Kruse developed the project by using complex, highly differentiated dynamic systems of internal divisions. The application of standard plywood panels as the smallest modular element has been used throughout the project's construction. The dimensions of the triple-ply panels dictate the rhythm of the skeleton framework. The nursery school's inside and outside walls are made of the same materials, which strengthens the effect of homogeneity and simplicity. There are parallels in this with the present-day relevance of minimalism, such as the minimalism of the sculptor Donald Judd, or with the functional architecture of Heinrich Tessenow. Permanence and modernity are interlinked in the project's conception.

The differently structured wooden surfaces and the uniform gaps of a third-of-an-inch, wherever joints have had to be made in the woodwork, are Kruse's subtle way of underlining the respective functions of the structural elements. Here, Kruse meets the ideal of material uniformity, an ideal, which plays an important role in architecture, and not just in modern architecture. This uniformity of material heightens the sensation of space: the more homogeneous the surrounding space-defining surfaces are, the more they convey the impression of the space. It is also an intellectual design challenge, because it proves that it is possible to create an infinite number of different shapes and spaces with just one material, albeit processed into different structural elements (glue-laminated beams and uprights, and plywood panels).

Left: Foyer and stairs

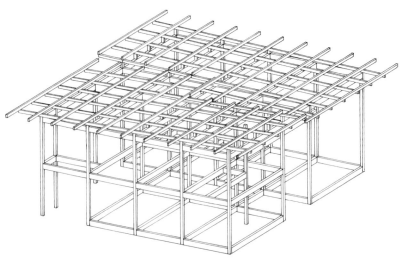

Top left: Small rumpus
room

Top right: Skeleton
framework

Above: Staircase

Right: Foyer and stairs

Opposite: Main rumpus
room

Above: Restroom
Photography: Tomas Riehle

Oliver Kruse
Raketenstation Hombroich
D-41472 Neuss
Germany
Telephone: +49 2182 18492
Facsimile: +49 2182 18492
Email: O.Kruse@gmx.de

Oliver Kruse was born in Germany in 1965. He trained as a joiner, studied sculpture in 1986, and was assistant to Erwin Heerich in Düsseldorf until 1991. Kruse continued his studies in London and received a masters degree in fine art and sculpture at Chelsea College of Art in 1993. In 1994, he established a studio at Raketenstation, Hombroich, where he was involved in the renovation and architectural transformation of this former military site.

Kruse has been a member of the board of the Insel Hombroich Foundation since 1996. He has exhibited in numerous group and solo exhibitions and has also been commissioned for public art and architectural projects, winning BDA awards in 1997, 2000, and 2001. Kruse now lives and works in Cologne and Hombroich in Germany.

Panacea Nightclub

Detroit, Michigan, USA

McIntosh Poris Associates

The juxtaposition of archeology and techno creates new life in re-emerging downtown Detroit. The developers envisioned a vibrant nightclub in this 1924 bank building to attract a diverse clientele.

They sought a space that would be arranged around a large dance floor but which would still offer both public and private spaces. Techno DJs and musicians would oversee the action and channel the mood.

The architects' solution embraced the existing original elements. What was not readily apparent was uncovered through careful archeology. The most prized find was the building's original suspended plaster ceiling with its hand-stenciled detailing that covers two-thirds of the space.

The space revolves around the dance floor so people are visually connected to the musicians. Spatial variety is maintained as people can move away from the dance floor to sit or stand in different lounges at the edges of the space. In so doing, they add to the atmosphere as they pass by scrim curtains, perforated metal panels, and frosted glass sheets, all of which filter their actions while providing a glimpse of their movement. Coordinated lighting schemes shine on and through these filtering elements, making them double as projection materials. Thus, people and light combine to enhance the layering throughout the space.

On the mezzanine level, the former bank manager's office became the perfect solution for situating DJs and lighting technicians, who mix and watch the dance floor action through the office's original glass window. Above, the hand-stenciled ceiling adds warmth to the interior surfaces and materials, which also include concrete floors, steel handrails, and glass partitions.

Left: Dance floor occupies main double-height space

Above: Colored lighting
and banquettes define
mezzanine-level lounge

Panacea Nightclub

Above: Dramatic lighting effects highlight bar and dance floor

Left: Lounge area surrounds central dance floor

Above: Industrial materials
mix with vibrant, techno
colors and surfaces

Photography: Laszlo Regos

McIntosh Poris Associates

1249 Washington Boulevard
Suite 1400
Detroit, MI, 48226
USA
Tel: +1 313 961 0601
Fax: +1 313 961 0652
Email: mporis@mcintoshporis.com

McIntosh Poris Associates provides architectural, interior, and urban design services to institutional, commercial, and residential clients. The firm's goal is to transform cities into more livable communities and urban centers, with architectural solutions arrived at through vision and dialogue. Both Doug McIntosh and

Michael Poris received Bachelor of Science degrees in Architecture from University of Michigan. Poris earned a Masters of Architecture at the Southern California Institute of Architecture; McIntosh received a Masters of Architecture from Yale University.

Pinakothek Modern

Munich, Germany

Stephan Braunfels Architects

The Pinakothek Modern in Munich is built next to the Old and New Pinakothek on the former site of the Turkish Barracks. Its location provides a link between the rigid 'chessboard' grid of the Maxvorstadt neighborhood and the irregular urban-planning scheme of the old city center.

The museum's main entrance is on the building's northwest side, facing both the Old and New Pinakothek. However, visitors arriving from city center can also enter through a large conservatory on the southeast side. All of the museum's internal circulation routes start and end in the building's rotunda. A large staircase corresponds with the entrance's line of sight and connects the museum's three main levels in a single flight in the form of an oversized trapezoid.

Columns of light around the rotunda visually join all exhibition levels and allow daylight to penetrate the whole building, right down to the basement. The exhibition galleries are rectangular or square-shaped, in various proportions appropriate to the works of art they display. Simple white-rendered walls and a terrazzo floor finish ensure that visitors focus on the artwork being displayed in the galleries.

The entire upper floor of the museum with its seemingly endless sequence of rooms is lit exclusively by daylight. The skylight glazing is designed in such a way as to make the exhibition galleries look higher than they actually are and to illuminate the galleries as evenly as possible. Views to the exterior punctuate the smaller exhibition spaces between the galleries on the upper floor and through high studio windows in the galleries on the ground floor.

Left: State gallery of modern art

Above left: Rotunda

Above right: Stairs to wardrobes

Right: 'Circle and square'

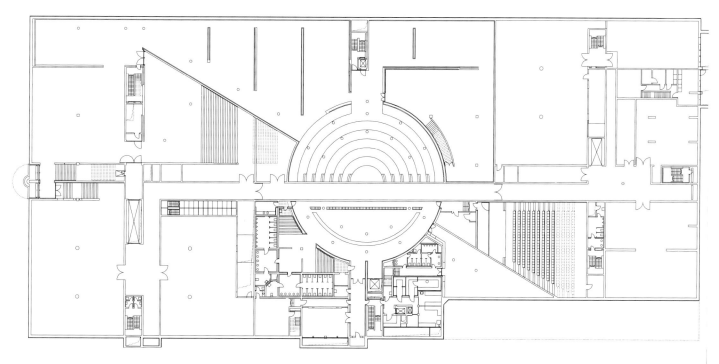

Left: Winter garden
Photography: Jens Weber

Stephan Braunfels Architects
Kochstrasse 60
10969 Berlin
Germany
Telephone: +49 30 253 7600
Facsimile: +49 30 2537 6050
Email: sba-berlin@braunfels-architekten.de

Stephan Braunfels was born in 1950 and completed his architectural studies at the Technical University of Munich in 1975. In 1978 he established his own firm, Stephan Braunfels Architects, in Munich.

The office regularly enters architectural competitions in both Germany and more broadly, with projects including the Museum for Art and Design in Ingolstadt, the Post Tower in Bonn, and the Science and Technical Museum in Cairo, Egypt. Major projects completed to date include the Pinakothek Modern in Munich, the Paul-Loebe Building for the German federal government in Berlin and a redevelopment/redesign of the Wilhelmshoehe Museum Palace in Kassel.

In 1996, Stephan Braunfels Architects opened its second office in Berlin.

Restaurant Azie

San Francisco, California, USA

CCS Architecture

Azie is a popular restaurant renowned for its French-Asian fusion menu, located in an urban infill space. Azie explores the restaurant as a public setting—a place that takes on its own life while creating individual opportunities to see, meet, and experience. Ten loft units, built above the restaurant, maximize the site's potential and further energize the Yerba Buena district.

Clubs and lounges from Paris to Hong Kong influenced Azie's design, which is spatially dramatic, yet intimate and tactile. A central, red-columned pavilion anchors the voluminous, double-height room. The surrounding spaces are tall and narrow, similar in proportion to a Chinatown streetscape. A two-story wall of mirrors and back-lit colored glass, installed at various angles, creates a cubist reflection of the room.

Opportunistic vistas—across, up, over, and down—emerge from the multi-level organization of the space. There are intimate zones within the more open volume, each distinctive for its location and function. The curved stairway is a sculptural element with kinetic action that links the floors together.

Left: Dining mezzanine looking towards mezzanine bar and kitchen
Photography: David Duncan Livingston

Above: Restaurant entrance/façade at night
Photography: David Duncan Livingston

GROUND FLOOR PLAN
3/32" = 1'-0"

Above: Ground-floor plan

Right: Mezzanine dining over private dining booths with curtains

Photography: David Duncan Livingston

Above: Double-height space
with dining pavilion and
mirrored wall

Photography: Michael O'Callahan

Restaurant Azie

Left: Stairs with bar beyond
Photography: David Duncan Livingston

CCS Architecture

44 McLea Court
San Francisco, California, 94103
USA
Tel: 415 864 2800
Fax: 415 864 2850
Email: info@ccs-architecture.com

CCS Architecture, the design studio of Cass Calder Smith, is dedicated to excellence in Architecture and Design. Since it's inception in 1990, CCS has designed a diverse range of public and private buildings and interiors for living, working, eating, and more. The firm has gained international acclaim for the architectural and commercial success of restaurant projects, while the uniqueness of residential, commercial, and mixed-use projects has met with an unusual degree of owner satisfaction and media praise.

CCS seeks to explore opportunities of maximum potential and express them at a scale appropriate to each project. The work is firmly based in the modernist idiom where innovation and creativity are balanced by common sense and experience. The firm is known for creating projects with exceptional spatial and material qualities, and for providing outstanding professional service.

Scharnhauser Park Town Hall

Ostfildern, Germany

J. Mayer H.

Stadt.haus is located at the center of Scharnhauser Park, a former military site next to Stuttgart Airport. As a multifunctional public building it unifies space for municipal administration, civil services, a public library, an art gallery, classrooms for music lessons, an evening school, a wedding room, office spaces, sports facilities, and a multipurpose hall. The combination of different public services generates a synergy and programmatic and visual transparency. Spatially, the entire building is a large and open public space with inlays of certain core elements.

Floating within a space for mutual or strategic communication, these enclosed 'boxes' structure the building's interior layout from the main square to the panorama deck on the roof, the stadt.haus interlocks with its context through cutouts and terraces. These open-air spaces remain accessible beyond the main opening hours and therefore serve as spatial and programmatic extensions.

Animated light and water features are an integral part of the stadt.haus and create a subtle reference to the relationship between nature and technology. Framing the main entrance, visitors walk through computer-animated artificial rain dripping from the underside of the flat cantilevered roof. The stadt.haus and square construct a new public building prototype by offering city life in real, mediated and virtual space.

Below: Art gallery stairs

Above: Art gallery

Above right: Door to atrium stair

Right: Section through atrium

Below: Multipurpose hall

Opposite: Atrium staircase

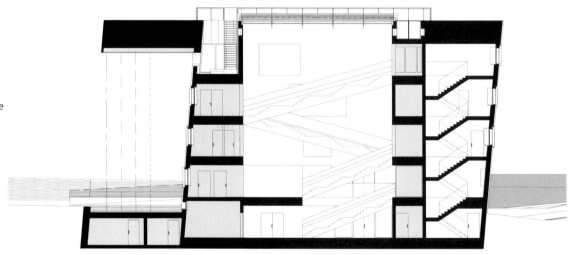

Scharnhauser Park Town Hall

J. Mayer H.
Bleibtreustrasse 54
10623 Berlin
Germany
Tel: +49 30 3150 6117
Fax: +49 30 3150 6118
Email: contact@jmayerh.de

Founded in 1996 in Berlin, Germany, J. Mayer H. works at the intersection of architecture, communication, and new technology. Recent projects include the Ostfildern Townhall, Germany, the Heat.Seat (a range of thermosensitive lounge furniture), the masterplan for Potsdam Docklands 2002, and two residential constructions in Berlin.

From urban planning schemes and buildings to installation work and objects, the relationship between the human body, technology, and nature form the background for a new production of space.

Jurgen Mayer H. is founder and principal of this multidisciplined studio. He has studied at Stuttgart University, The Cooper Union, and at Princeton University, and his work has been published and exhibited worldwide. Collections such as the MoMa New York and SF MoMa feature his work. He has taught at both Harvard and the Arts University of Berlin.

School

Paspels, Switzerand

Valerio Olgiati

One would scarcely suspect that the client of this school building was the community of a mountain village with a population of 400. Designed with clear, simple lines, the structure forms a striking contrast to similar projects in the area. It is distinguished by an economic exploitation of the site and by the use of materials familiar to agricultural buildings in the region.

The three-story structure in exposed concrete rises like an outcrop of rock from the alpine meadows. The different treatment of the circulation routes and the functional areas is reflected externally in the façade. At those points where corridors or staircases occur internally, the fenestration is flush with the outer wall surface. The cruciform layout of the circulation system allows the ingress of daylight from all directions, which results in changing spatial impressions during the course of the day.

In contrast to the corridors and staircases, which are entirely in exposed concrete, the classrooms are lined internally with wood. Here, the long window strips are set flush with the inner face of the wall and frame distinct views of the surroundings. The concrete internal walls and the floor slabs, designed as a monolithic structure, form an independent load-bearing framework that is tied to the exposed concrete envelope by shear connector pins. All abutments between walls and floors are articulated with shadow joints.

Above: View from corridor toward
outside and staircase

Photography: Valerio Olgiati

Opposite: View from corridor
Photography: Helfenstein Heinrich

Left: View from corridor
Photography: Valerio Olgiati

Below left: View from corridor
Photography: Valerio Olgiati

Below right: Door detail
Photography: Valerio Olgiati

Bottom: Section

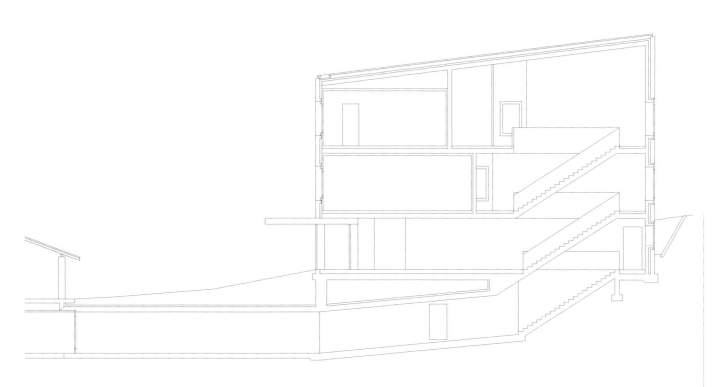

Above: Schoolroom
Photography: Helfenstein Heinrich

Valerio Olgiati
Hafnerstrasse 60
CH-8005 Zurich
Switzerland
Telephone: +41 1 440 5161
Facsimile: +41 1 440 5162
Email: mail@olgiati.net

Valerio Olgiati, born in 1958, practices and resides in Zurich, Switzerland. He was educated at the ETH Zurich, and set up his sole practice two years after his graduation in 1988. The firm's most distinguished projects include a cultural center in Films, Switzerland and the alpine school in Paspels, Switzerland. He has lectured and run studio workshops as a visiting professor at the Technical University, Stuttgart and more recently at the ETH Zurich.

Small Plates Restaurant
Detroit, Michigan, USA

McIntosh Poris Associates

Small Plates is a neighborhood restaurant and bar that seats 80 people. The restaurant is located on the ground floor of Detroit's Eureka Building, which was recently converted into residential lofts by McIntosh Poris.

The client wanted a new restaurant with an open kitchen, a brick oven, and a comfortable, warm neighborhood feeling.

Employing a strategy of 'revealing and editing,' the architects created an inviting space that highlights the building's urban, industrial history while serving as an intimate, relaxed space. Pushing the glass-paned façade out to the original street frontage has engaged passersby and creates a strong street presence. Visible from the street, the restaurant's bright yellow walls and warm oak floors welcome visitors into the restaurant.

The dining room is 18 by 60 foot and has a 7 by 10 foot stained plywood bar on one side, and on the other a banquette covered in crypton, an easy to maintain industrial fabric with a soft, suede-like feel. Just beyond the banquette, the brick oven is visible to diners, hinting at the kitchen beyond. In addition to the large banquette, small café tables fill the dining area.

The designers left much of the existing structure from the vacant space intact and exposed, including the original plaster and concrete structure. Stained plywood, wood floors, yellow, red and green paint on the walls and black paint on the ceiling create warmth and spatial unity.

Prints of building fragments from New York-based artist Esteban Chávez reinforce the building's industrial character and historic past.

Left: Warm colors mix with industrial materials in restaurant's interior

Above: Glass façade
creates inviting,
neighborhood feeling

Below: Artwork features
architectural details and
building fragments

Opposite: Plywood host's
desk and upholstered
banquette frame dining
room

Small Plates Restaurant

Above: View across bar to
brick oven and kitchen
beyond

Photography: Laszlo Regos

McIntosh Poris Associates

1249 Washington Boulevard
Suite 1400
Detroit, MI, 48226
USA
Tel: +1 313 961 0601
Fax: +1 313 961 0652
Email: mporis@mcintoshporis.com

McIntosh Poris Associates provides architectural, interior, and urban design services to institutional, commercial, and residential clients. The firm's goal is to transform cities into more livable communities and urban centers with architectural solutions arrived at through vision and dialogue. Both Doug McIntosh and

Michael Poris received Bachelor of Science degrees in Architecture from University of Michigan. Poris earned a Masters of Architecture at the Southern California Institute of Architecture; McIntosh received a Masters of Architecture from Yale University.

Town Hall Gallery

Innsbruck, Austria

Dominique Perrault

Both civic and private entrepreneurs developed a brief for the construction of the new Innsbruck town hall. The brief included the preservation of the old buildings, the remodeling of a vegetated public square, a hotel opening onto the public square, and the linking of the entire complex by a network of public circulation spaces and covered galleries, and the creation of a lower-ground shopping area with both fast-food outlets and traditional restaurants.

Such a prominent public site required various construction stages. The overall project fills a city block, but also features diverse interrelated elements to create an urban landscape and a new city skyline. A glass bell tower emerges above the design to converse with other nearby bell towers.

Other features, apart from the bell tower, also make the town hall stand out. The city council chamber is placed on the roof in a 'rooftop house.' Above the hotel, the rooftop garden includes a restaurant that opens to sweeping views of the surrounding mountains. One old patio covers a market-style shopping area, while another patio features tree plantings to create an indoor garden. A glass-covered passageway becomes the backbone of the project.

The project collates and organizes the diverse types of architecture like a sedimentation of lines that bears witness to each period. The identity lives in the material chosen and the architectural language in each section. Glass, transparent or white, translucent or colored, becomes a reference material. The window carpentry is thick or thin depending on whether it is fixed or hinged.

The architectural language is Mondrian. Unlike painting, in architecture, 'pure' does not exist as a concept. The buildings are clad in metal cloth, sun shading or visual protection, creating different sheens and different types of light. In other words, it creates a different complexity which creates a modern hybrid architecture, thus reflecting the history of the site, which like European culture, is a mixture of abstraction and figuration, trade and politics, culture and leisure.

Left: Stairwell atrium

Above: Detail of glass façade

Above right & right: Shadow play of glass façade with artwork by Peter Kogler

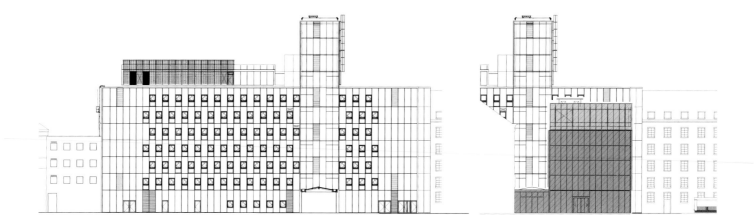

Above: Glass façade
Photography: Roland Halbe

Dominique Perrault

26, Rue Bruneseau
Paris 75629
France
Telephone: +33 1 4406 0000
Facsimile: +33 1 4406 0001
Email: dominique.perrault@perraultarchitecte.com

Dominique Perrault received his architecture degree in Paris in 1978 and his certificate in town planning at the Ecole nationale des Ponts et Chaussées in 1979.

His work is extremely varied and includes many new constructions and numerous renovations. The architectural programs of these projects range from large buildings, such as cultural or sports projects, to smaller projects, such as urban 'insertions' in blighted urban areas to private housing in prestigious neighborhoods.

Perrault has been awarded various prizes, notably the Great National Prize of Architecture in 1996 and the Mies van der Rohe Prize for the National Library in France in 1997.

Dominique Perrault is Chevalier of the Legion of Honor, member of the Architecture Academy, honorable member of the German Association of Architects (BDA) and of the British Royal Institute of Architecture (RIA). From November 1998 to February 2001 he was President of the French Institute of Architects.

Dominique Perrault is currently an architectural consultant for the mayor of Barcelona.

Typhoon Restaurant and The Hump

Santa Monica, California, USA

SFJones Architects, Inc

The Hump Sushi Bar and *Typhoon* are both Brian Vidor restaurants that occupy prime viewing space at the Santa Monica Airport. Stephen Jones worked with architects Grienstien/Daniels on *Typhoon* in the early 1990s. The general image associated with a 'typhoon' is central in the restaurant's design, first as a weather pattern specific the western rim of the Pacific, and also as a map symbol recognizable to aviators. Seating is oriented towards the glazed façade overlooking the airport taxiway, but the bar is positioned so that the bartender greets patrons on arrival.

The success of *Typhoon* encouraged Brian Vidor to commission Stephen Jones to design *The Hump Sushi Bar*. Many US pilots in World War II followed a famous flight path from India to China over the Himalayas known as 'The Hump.' Vidor also envisaged a restaurant with a wider influence than Japan, noting from his personal travel experiences that sushi was a part of other culture's food experiences. As such, the food preparation area is like a stage purposefully designed to display the skill of the sushi chefs.

A pebble path guides patrons into the restaurant's entrance past the fresh seafood displays, with views to the Los Angeles skyline above the food display through an elegant glass wall. Randomly positioned bamboo struts hold up seaweed grass matting to create a ceiling. The front doors, maître d stand and cabinets are artefacts imported from India which have been manipulated to serve their new function. Light fixtures were chosen to reinforce the design and to give reference to the airport (the ceiling fans looked like airplane propellers, and a small plane with a light was part of the track light at the entrance).

Left: View from the Hump's dining room towards sushi bar and etched-glass mural of Mt Everest

Photography: Anthony Perez

Above: Typhoon dining
room with view towards
runway
Photography: Tim Street Porter

Below: View from The
Hump towards runway
showing seaweed and
bamboo ceiling
Photography: Anthony Perez

Above: Fireplace in The Hump's dining room
Photography: Anthony Perez

Left:Entrance to The Hump in foreground showing some items imported from India— door, maitre d' stand
Photography: Anthony Perez

Below: Main bar of Typhoon, backlit weather map mural behind bar
Photography: Tim Street Porter

Above: The Hump Sushi
Bar with view towards
runway and ocean

Photography: Anthony Perez

SFJones Architects, Inc
4218 Glencoe Avenue
Studio Two
Marina Del Rey, California, 90292
USA
Tel: +1 310 822 3822
Fax: +1 310 306 4441
Email: mailbox@sfjones.com

Stephen Jones has a solid reputation as architect and designer, flowing from his intense passion for work. From California to Japan, Jones' resume is as impeccable as it is varied, and a host of new projects promise to live up to his high standard of excellence and expand his reputation.

Jones and his seven employees remain dedicated to their well-established niche of designing restaurants, in which the firm focuses on the importance of the melding of function and aesthetics.

Jones is quick to credit the others at his firm and the legion of craftspeople and specialists they work with in developing and keeping their stellar reputation; indeed, SFJones Architects, Inc. is able to provide meticulous attention to every project. All aspects of each project are designed and coordinated by the firm. The firm's offices reflect this, and are more reminiscent of an artisan's workshop than a high-tech 'building factory.'

Currently, the firm's works in progress include projects for Grill Concepts, Lucky Strike, and a continuous turnover of hospitality and residential projects.

Wildwood Secondary Campus

Los Angeles, California, USA

SPF:a

In an American high school culture characterized by a low level of expectation and a fragmented educational experience, the proposal for this project sought to reformulate a high school institution within a recycled urban context. This approach involved planning on two functional fronts. The first was that the project should exploit the student's ability to learn laterally and vertically through seemingly unconnected subjects to achieve holistic knowledge. The campus layout delineates these interdisciplinary relationships. The second was that one of Wildwood's stated goals is the student's ability to graduate as a part of the community.

The existing building was a single-story light manufacturing building constructed around 1940. Our proposal was designed not to alter the structure, but rather to create freestanding program components within the shell of the building. The solution is straightforward because it utilizes the building's existing geometry. Space was 'found' in the center upper portion of each truss bay, which was utilized for student portfolio storage, lounge spaces, and art studios.

The project encourages interdisciplinary learning by grouping math, language, and humanities classes around an open common space with a stair. The notion of flexible space was also deployed throughout the project. For instance, the theater, music room, and gathering space are clustered near one another and systems of operable doors are used to separate and join spaces as needed.

At the senior level, students are encouraged to work and conduct independent study within the community. On a social level, the street orientation of the layout locates the gathering spaces to allow outside community participation with the students.

Left: Administration and parking entrance on north side

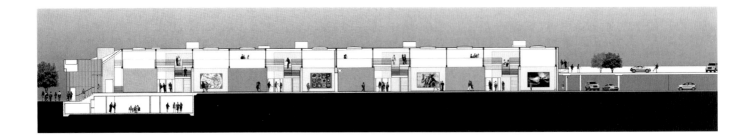

Above: Longitudinal section looking towards four pods

Below left: Exploded assembly axonometric

Below right: Student and school gallery space

Bottom right: Flexible theater space with gathering space beyond

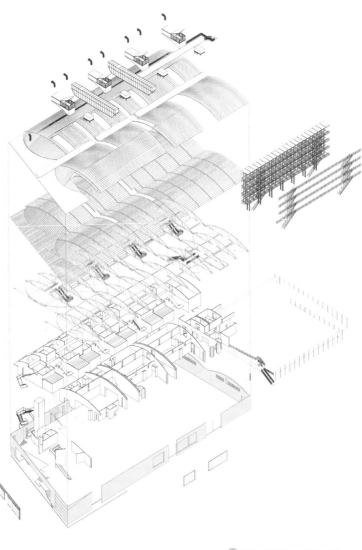

 EXISTING STRUCTURE

Above: Student art gallery/reception area with skylights
and east-facing store-front windows

SPF:a
3384 Robertson Place
Second Floor
Los Angeles, CA 90034
USA
Telephone: +1 310 558 0902
Facsimile: +1 310 558 0904
Email: stenfors@SPFa.com

The shared vision of the firm's principals, Jeffrey Stenfors, Zoltan Pali and Judit Fekete emanates from the visibly technological and conceptual possibilities for the future of architecture.

Uninspired by theory, SPF:a explores ideas through the realities of construction and by solving the problem at hand. In the firm's search for new solutions through inventive design, it does not specialize in any one building type due to the belief that creativity is the product of diversity rather than repetition. Instead, the practice's philosophy embodies a continuous search for new, fresh solutions. Each problem has its own best solution, which is not a derivation of another problem.

SPF:a is mainly concerned with the quality and originality of each project within the needs, budgets, and schedules of those with whom its staff work. The firm takes pride in its commitment to architecture, for which its peers have given recognition.

SPF:a has a staff of 40 professionals and provides services in urban design, programming and feasibility studies, site selection, analysis and use, energy conservation, tenant improvement, building renovation, and graphic design.

Zibibbo

Palo Alto, California, USA
CCS Architecture

Zibibbo is a sister restaurant to LuLu in San Francisco. The 14,000-square-foot, 400-seat restaurant is a casual place with a variety of indoor and outdoor spaces that enable its patrons to bask in the gentle peninsula climate. Like the menu, the design is reminiscent of the Mediterranean—from Southern France to Morocco, Spain, and Italy.

Occupying the length of a city block, Zibibbo is organized along a yellow-brick road that links three buildings, as well as dining gardens set with olive trees, aromatic herbs, flowers, and fountains. The first building is a Victorian building from the 1890s that was transformed into the restaurant's main bar. The second building, built to house the main dining room, has an industrial barrel-vaulted roof, and is oriented to extend into the adjacent gardens via slide-away glass doors on either end.

The third building, a renovated double-story commercial structure, features two floors of dining and a bustling, open kitchen. The mezzanine overlooks the tremendous working kitchen, a frenzy of oak fires, burners, and rotisseries. Where this building meets the street, there is a modern French-Italian sidewalk café and wine bar. Alongside the café is the 'gallery,' a long dining room with a collection of photography exhibited within full-height paneled walls.

Left: Mezzanine view of open kitchen

Below: Ground floor and
mezzanine-level plans

Bottom: Main dining room
with axis through to
second façade

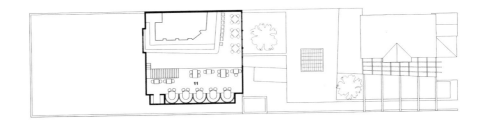

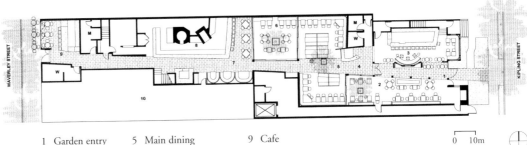

1 Garden entry	5 Main dining	9 Cafe
2 Garden #1	6 Garden #2	10 Existing tenent space
3 Bar/dining	7 Kitchen dining	11 Mezzanine dining
4 Main entry	8 Exhibition kitchen	

0   10m

Above: Café/bar dining at second façade

Left: Main dining room leading through to garden

Right: Axis through open kitchen
Photography: Michael Bruk

CCS Architecture
44 McLea Court
San Francisco, California, 94103
USA
Tel: 415-864-2800
Fax: 415-864-2850
Email: info@ccs-architecture.com

CCS Architecture, the design studio of Cass Calder Smith, is dedicated to excellence in Architecture and Design. Since it's inception in 1990, CCS has designed a diverse range of public and private buildings and interiors for living, working, eating, and more. The firm has gained international acclaim for the architectural and commercial success of restaurant projects, while the uniqueness of residential, commercial, and mixed-use projects has met with an unusual degree of owner satisfaction and media praise.

CCS seeks to explore opportunities of maximum potential and express them at a scale appropriate to each project. The work is firmly based in the modernist idiom where innovation and creativity are balanced by common sense and experience. The firm is known for creating projects with exceptional spatial and material qualities, and for providing outstanding professional service.

ZOOM Children's Museum

Vienna, Austria

pool Architects

Viennese firm, pool Architects was commissioned to design a children's museum for the city's newly adapted Museum Quarter. After demolishing the former imperial horse stable and coal shelter interiors, all that remained was exposed brickwork. A complete loss of identity resulted from stripping the original spaces: edges, niches, spikes—everything had been removed.

The firm viewed its role, on the one hand, to fulfill the given requirements by creating an entrance hall, auditorium, exhibition area, an atelier, and to equip the multimedia ZOOM-lab with the necessary structural and technical infrastructure. On the other hand, it was important to charge the old brickwork emotionally with purposeful interventions. These interventions manipulate the existing building by providing a backdrop to the museum's interior. A humane, down-to-earth space that visitors can enjoy, and that simply melts into the background of the museum's function.

Below: Entrance hall and reception desk with locker furniture in foreground

Top: Gallery reading and relaxation area

Above: Lecture table in auditorium

Above: Reception desk in entrance hall

Left: Rendering of entire museum

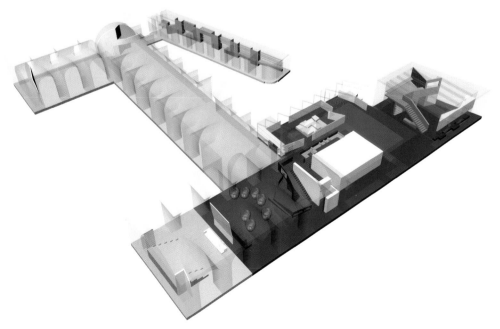

Above: Multimedia zoom lab

Left: Entrance hall with closet storage

Photography: Hertha Hurnaus

pool Architects
Weyringergasse 36/1
A-1040 Vienna
Austria
Telephone: +43 1 5038 2310
Facsimile: +43 1 5038 23133
Email: pool@helma.at

pool Architects are Evelyn Rudnicki, Christoph Lammerhuber, Axel Linemayr and Florian Wallnöfer. The group began collaborating 1989 in what was to become the BKK-2 team of architects, formed in 1993, together with other members. In 1998, pool Architects was established.

An essential feature of pool's design approach, lies in the constant search for additional functional and emotional dimensions, and in mixing them with the original scope of work, in order to charge space with energy and potentiality otherwise unknown.

Currently, pool is working on a variety of projects ranging from a rooftop remodeling to several office and apartment buildings, and urban development schemes and strategies. To strengthen activity in the field of urban research, iPool—an institute for analysis, trends, and urbanization—has been created with Manfred Schenekl.

Residential

64 Wakefield

Atlanta, Georgia, USA

Mack Scogin Merrill Elam Architects

Formerly Scogin, Elam and Bray Architects

The site, which is small with a shared driveway, fronts south looking across the street toward the neighborhood park, swimming pool, and tennis courts in the valley, and a nature reserve on the hill beyond. The idea of a lap pool drove the design process—dreams of exercise and relaxation, recollections of the Josephine Baker house, and visions of the Italian rationalists' health clinics.

Only the 70-foot width of the site afforded the necessary length for the pool so it was located on the second floor, spanning the spaces of the floor below and gathering in the south light. Shielded from the street by a translucent glass wall but open to the sky and air, the roof deck and pool challenge the very notion of 'public' and 'private.' Outside the site passersby can hear the splashing of people in the pool. Inside, one can tell which neighbor is walking their dog by the sound of its collar and leash. No swimsuit is required.

The pool is constructed of poured-in-place reinforced concrete with a plaster lining. The house is a wood-frame structure with stucco and glass enclosing surfaces. Interior materials include painted gypsum wallboard and cementitions.

Below: Stair looking towards master bedroom and pool beyond

Below: North-south section
looking east

Bottom: View from living
space towards stair and
pool

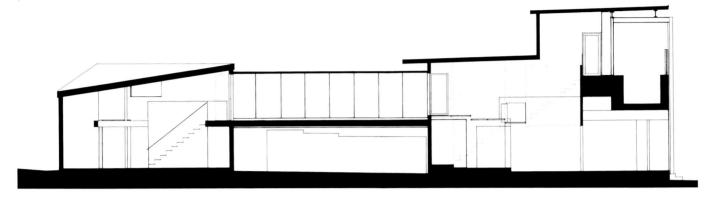

Top: Living space

Above left: Living space

Above: Master bedroom

Above: Pool and master
bedroom
Photography: Timothy Hursley

Mack Scogin Merrill Elam Architects

75 J.W. Dobbs Avenue
Atlanta, Georgia, 30303
USA
Telephone: +1 404 525 6869
Facsimile: +1 404 525 7061
Email: office@msmearch.com

Mack Scogin and Merrill Elam, the two principals of Mack Scogin Merrill Elam Architects have worked together in architecture for over 30 years. The firm, formerly known as Scogin Elam and Bray, was formed in order to take full advantage of the complimentary skills and talents of the two principals.

Projects by Mack Scogin and Merrill Elam have received over 40 design awards, including five National American Institute of Architects Awards of Excellence. Together they received the 1995 Academy Award in Architecture from the American Academy of Arts and Letters and the 1996 Chrysler Award for Innovation in Design.

Mack Scogin and Merrill Elam have had the privilege to work with some of the most prestigious and respected clients in the world. Project types include office buildings, factories, stadia, airports, health facilities, houses, dormitories, classroom and studio facilities, campus centers, libraries, museums, galleries, exhibitions, schools, warehouses and jails, among others.

Current and recent projects include the Wang Campus Center and Davis Garage for Wellesley College in Massachusetts; the United States Federal Courthouse in Austin, Texas; a School of Architecture for The Ohio State University in Columbus, Ohio; a Music Library for The University of California at Berkeley in California, and the Herman Miller Cherokee Operations facility in Canton, Georgia.

Alvano Residence

Hamburg, Germany

gmp Architects

The site for the Alvano Residence was created by sub-dividing a city park. The location of the building at the eastern boundary maintains the park's generous proportions and dimension as far as possible.

Inside the house, a double-story-height entrance hall visually connects both living levels, while offering wall space for the presentation of artwork. Sliding elements on the ground floor can be used to open up this level into a generous space.

The residence's interior finish is designed with Duralit industrial floor covering, clear glazed fair-faced concrete ceilings, plastered walls, steel windows, steel balustrades, and marble in the bathrooms.

To illuminate the home's interior, the east, south, and north façades include several window openings, while the west façade opens up completely toward the garden. Easy-to-slide shading elements form screens of Corten steel strips, which can be positioned according to the changing angle of the sun with each season.

Left: Glass walls

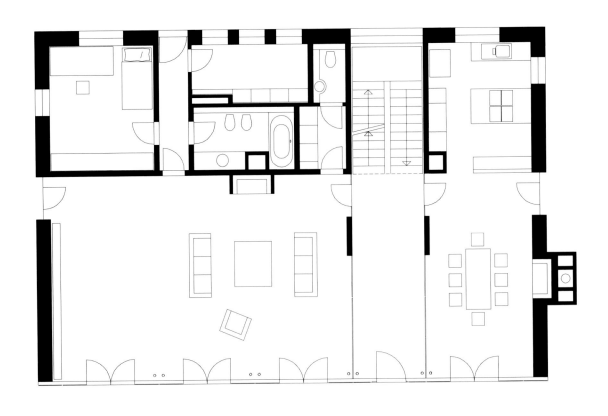

Above: Lower floor plan

Right: Play of light produced by sliding steel screens

Above left: Stair connecting both living levels

Above right: Glass walls

Left: View from dining into kitchen

Above: View from living to
entrance hall and dining

Photography: Klaus Frahm

gmp Architects
von Gerkan, Marg und Partner
Elbchaussee 139
22763 Hamburg
Germany
Telephone: +49 4088 1510
Facsimile: +49 4088 151177
Email: hamburg-e@gmp-architekten.de

gmp Architects was established in 1965. Since then, Meinhard von Gerkan, Volkwin Marg, and their partners have planned and constructed a broad range of buildings. The firm is internationally recognized for its completed projects, such as the airports in Berlin, Stuttgart, and Hamburg, and the New Trade Fair in Leipzig. Currently, projects under construction include the New Lehrter Central Station in Berlin, the reconstruction of the Berlin Olympic Stadium, and the International Convention and Exhibition Centre in Nanning, China.

Ann Street Loft 6

Sydney, Australia

Dale Jones-Evans Pty Ltd

This project is located in part of the Ann Street Warehouse Conversion redevelopment in Surry Hills in Sydney, where the architect purchased a standard apartment and then replanned it and fitted it out. While aspects of the inherited plan were unnegotiable, the main points of departure were to incorporate one of the bedrooms into the general living space, and to re-detail most aspects of the interior.

The approach was to restructure the ground plane as a cavernous sinew of spaces and make the floor solid, so that one feels grounded. The three-story void was employed as the circulatory space between the floors by cantilevering and floating the main stairs and using slatted timbers for landings and bridges.

The interior utilizes a painterly palette of surfaces to offset the owner's art collection. The functional division of the space between sleeping and living areas generates the off-white to black-brown color scheme in the development. The spaces on the lower floor are cave-like and white, while the upper floors are painted off-black as a contrast to the solid-white cavern below.

The dark ceiling and floor in the living spaces tempers the intensity of the east–west light, visually extending the space toward the external deck and water-garden. The water-garden is replenished through a talon of copper as part of a cooling and decorative device for the living spaces.

In the sunroom on the roof level, light is filtered through a bamboo screen to reinforce the presence of light and sky. The roof level acts as a place in which to connect with nature and for contemplation, while offering spectacular views of downtown Sydney.

Above: Main bedroom with curved wall and gallery/robe

Photography: Jeremy Simons

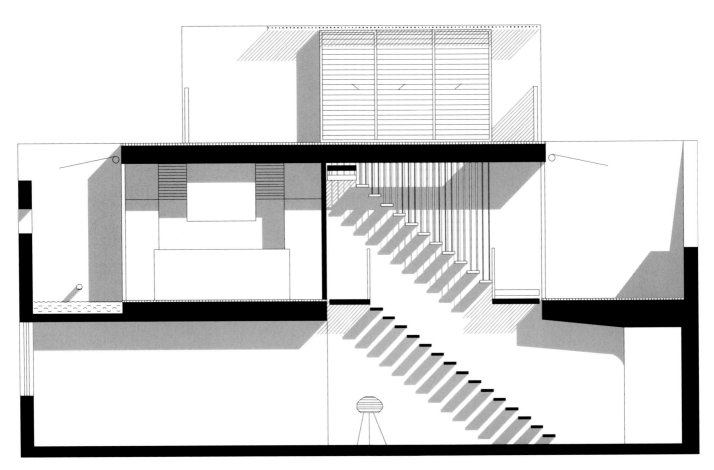

Top: East-west section

Above: Black-pebbled pool
with copper talon

Photography: Willem
Rethmeier

Right: Living room/kitchen

Photography: Giorgio Possenti

Below: Entry gallery and
floating stairs
Photography: Giorgio Possenti

Above: Caved entry with
Indian light Jalis

Photography: Jeremy Simons

Dale Jones-Evans Pty Ltd
Loft 1, 50-54 Ann Street
Surry Hills, New South Wales, 2010
Australia
Telephone: +61 2 9211 0626
Facsimile: +61 2 9211 5998
Email: dje@dje.com.au

Dale Jones-Evans is well known for his innovative approach and contribution to the development of art and architecture in Australia. He has studied painting and architecture and has been in private practice since 1983.

Jones-Evans has received an international residential award in America and numerous Australian awards including the prestigious Royal Australian Institute of Architects Robin Boyd Award in 1991, and more recently the 2001 Most Outstanding Residential Award in Western Australia and the 2002 National *Belle Magazine* 'House of the Year' Award.

He has exhibited in and curated many architecture and design exhibitions around Australia, including at the Centre for Contemporary Art in Melbourne and The National Gallery of Victoria. Dale Jones-Evans has taught and lectured on architecture and urban design at Royal Melbourne Institute of Technology, University of Melbourne, University of Sydney, and University of New South Wales. The office has a high media profile, with projects published regularly both in Australia and internationally.

Bergamo Loft
Bergamo, Italy
Attilio Stocchi Architecture Studio

The Loft outside Bergamo was converted from a disused factory building. Two bays of the six-bay factory have been used for the loft conversion to create a space of 1100 square feet with a further 400 square feet of intermediate levels.

The living, dining, and kitchen areas are located on the ground floor. A spiral staircase reaches the bedroom, which has a walk-in wardrobe. The poles that pierce the horizontal planes of the loft space are designed in a deliberately asymmetrical manner, in order to create a sense of play within the space.

Left: Bedroom with cantilevered bed

Below: Structural poles

Opposite: Bathroom and
walk-in wardrobe

Left: Illumination of
sculpture

Below: Plan

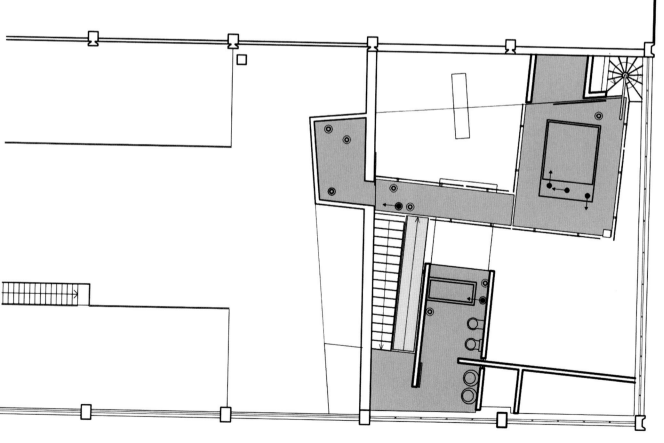

Below: Structural poles
Right: Dining table
Photography: Andrea Martiradonna

Attilio Stocchi Architecture Studio
Via Daverio 7
20122 Milano
Italy
Telephone: +39 2 5518 9184
Facsimile: +39 2 5518 9184
Email: z.rem@flashnet.it

Attilio Stocchi was born in Venice in 1965 and graduated from the Politecnico di Milano in 1991. His professional activity focuses on two main concerns. The first is experimental in nature and relates to urban design, such as the Codussi Square project in Lenna (Bergamo), the Maj Square project in Schilpario (Bergamo), and the Libertà Square in Spirano (Bergamo). His second focus is on research concerned with space and animal metamorphosis. This research is based on the design of projects such as the Papilio in Rome, the Nautilus in Bernareggio (Milano), and the Fluxum exhibition held at Palazzo Reale in Milan. Attilio Stocchi has written several review articles for *Abitare* magazine, as well as two books: *Vittoriano Viganò, Etica Brutalista* (Testo&Immagine), and *Gio Ponti, Tre Ville Inventate* (Segesta).

Betzenberg Houses
Kaiserslautern, Germany

AV1 Architects
Butz Dujmovic Shanné Urig

The theme of 'architecture versus nature' stands for all of the important decisions of this project's planning, resulting in its ecologically sustainable design.

The houses' orientation to the south encourages maximum sunlight penetration into their volumes. Other ecological considerations are their roofs, which have high-gauge insulation. The buildings also have roof gardens, which improve the microclimate of the area where the development is located, by storing rain in a special layer of the roof. The surplus rainwater drains to the ground without adding to the municipal sewerage.

A flexible floor layout and design is acheived through open-plan floors. The communal planning and living this creates is in symbiosis with the development's natural setting, enhancing a direct relationship with the outside and with nature. Special care and emphasis has been given to energy-efficient solutions throughout the design and subsequent use of the building.

Above: Ground floor, House 2

Below left: Basement, House 2
Right: Bathroom, House 2
Bottom: Kitchen, House 4

Left: Upper floor, House 2

Above: Staircases, House 2

Bottom: Bathroom in basement, House 2

Above left: Staircase in living room, House 3

Above right: House 2 by night

Photography: Michael Heinrich

AV1 Architects
Butz Dujmovic Shanné Urig
Kanalstrasse 75
67655 Kaiserslautern
Germany
Telephone: +49 631 340 3141
Facsimile: +49 631 340 3143
Email: info@av1architekten.de

AV1 Architects was founded in 1991 by Jurgen Butz, Boris Dujmovic, Michael Schanné, and Albert Urig in Kaiserslautern, Germany. The firm specializes in high-end residential design, with an increasing number of recent commissions for commercial projects such as their Kaiserslautern ASB Hospital Emergency Room, completed in 2002, or the Kolbermoor College and Gym, completed in 2003. The firm has received several awards in Germany, including the Staatspries 2000 for their Betzenberger housing scheme.

Cordes Apartment

Herzebrock, Germany

drewes+strenge architekten

The complete remodelling of a conventionally laid-out attic apartment was a response to the client's desire for loft living. All possible non-load-bearing dividing walls contributed to an open, continuous plan. However, the centrally located staircase and bathroom were obstacles in fully achieving this layout but they helped, instead, with the organization of the loft's different functional elements.

The demolition of the former ceiling above the living and dining areas allowed for generous vertical space and offered the option of locating a study gallery on the second level. This is accessible by a minimalist steel staircase. The kitchen is located in the center of the loft and acts as a hinge between the living and sleeping areas.

Visual connections in the apartment exist diagonally between the kitchen and the bed, and from the grand piano to the bathtub at the opposite end of the loft. Through this design, the sleeping and bathing areas are fully integrated into the open-plan living space and they are also immediately experienced on entering the loft. For privacy, a massive solid oak sliding door can separate the sleeping area from the rest of the space.

Below: Two black boxes conceal storage space and hide pitched roof

Opposite: Kitchen is hinge of loft space

Top: Countertop visually connects kitchen and living areas

Left: New steel beams also function as discreet light source

Above: Space unfolds with subtle variety of materials and textures

Left: Soft lighting defines
bathroom as relaxation zone

Below: Crisp steel stair
leads to study on mezzanine

Photographer: Christian Richters

drewes+strenge architekten

Bahnhofstrasse 10
D 33442 Herzebrock
Germany
Telephone: +49 5245 3208
Facsimile: +49 5245 18710
Email: frankdrewes@gmx.de

Frank Drewes was born in Herzebrock, Westphalia in 1963 and graduated from the Technical University of Aachen in 1991. He completed his Masters in architecture at the University of California, Berkeley in 1994. Since graduating, he has worked with a number of practices, including Arcquitectonica, Mark Mack, and Stanley Saitowitz in San Francisco. Martin Strenge was born in Gütersloh, Westphalia in 1963. He graduated from the Univeristy of Applied Sciences at Detmold in 1989. From 1989–99 Strenge worked with Professor Parade in Düsseldorf. In 1999, he co-founded the architecture firm Drewes+Strenge in Herzebrock, Westphalia.

GGG House
Mexico City, Mexico
Alberto Kalach Architect

The GGG House is conceived as a huge concrete monolith, fragmented geometrically within a spatial mesh, and defined by the repeated inscription of a sphere in a cube. Gardens, ponds, patios, pavilions, and alcoves communicate among themselves through the openings that break up the monolith into separate functional spaces.

The general volume of the house responds to its location, which is bordered by a golf course, a warehouse, and a five-story housing complex. Inside, light plays across the home's whitewashed walls. Rays of light filter through the openings; at times 'exploding' softly, flooding the interior spaces with light. Both shade and light enliven the passages through the house and contrast with the its open spaces, marking the flow of time.

Left: Shade and light enliven passages

Above: Interior and exterior communicate

Opposite: Bathroom—
house responds to its
location

Right: Gardens, ponds,
patios, and pavilions
communicate among
themselves

Below: Kitchen

Above: Television room
Photography: Jean-Luc Laloux

Alberto Kalach Architect
Gral F. Ramirez 17
Col Daniel Garza Tacu
Mexico City, 03720
Mexico
Email: alberto@kalach.com

Born in Mexico City, in 1960, Alberto Kalach studied architecture at Universidad Iberoamericana in Mexico City (1977–1981) and at Cornell University, New York, (1983–1985). He now lives and works in Mexico City and his concerns regarding the urban growth and redevelopment of this vast city are often reflected in his work. This ranges from his designs for minimalist houses to large-scale housing developments.

Kalach's view of architecture is made up of a series of reference points in the overall network that articulates the urban landscape. A building for him is a brick in the great work of collective architecture that we all create over time: the city.

Greenwich House

New York, USA

Hariri & Hariri

The main walls on the north and south of the house are enclosed by translucent fiberglass curtainwalls, occasionally interrupted by sections of clear glass. These walls act as a device to conceal and reveal at the same time, allowing the visitor a glimpse of life inside the private home. A virtual and actual transparency starting from the entrance hall continues within the house up to the master bedroom suite, which provides views out over the lawn.

Left: Bedroom

Opposite: Stair

Above: Staircase from entry landing

Left: Living

Greenwich House

235

Left: Entry and dining

Above: Dining

Photography: Jason Schmidt

Hariri & Hariri

18 East 12th Street #1C
New York, NY 10003
USA
Telephone: +1 212 727 0338
Facsimile: +1 212 727 0479
Email: info@haririandhariri.com

Hariri & Hariri was established in 1986 by Gisue Hariri and Mojgan Hariri. The two partners began their architectural collaboration early on, while still students at Cornell University, working together on various competitions. After graduation from Cornell and completion of their apprenticeship with distinguished architectural offices, the Iranian-born sisters set up their private practice in New York City, dedicated to innovative design.

House R 128
Stuttgart, Germany
Werner Sobek

This four-story building which was completed in 2000, occupies a steep parcel of land on the edge of the bowl-shaped valley in Stuttgart. The house was designed as a completely recyclable building, which produces no emissions and is self-sufficient in terms of energy requirements. Due to the mortise and tenon joints and bolted joints of its construction, the building cannot be assembled and dismantled easily, but it is recyclable. The building's electricity is produced by solar cells.

Access to the house is via a bridge leading to the top floor of the building's four levels. This floor accommodates the kitchen and dining area. The two levels below provide a living area and sleeping areas, while the lowest level accommodates the nursery and technical and utility installations. Each of the four levels is defined by a few pieces of furniture, in keeping with the concept of maximum transparency inside the building.

For the house to be an emission-free, zero-heating energy house, an innovative computer-controlled energy system was developed, which can be checked by telephone or computer. The solar energy, which radiates into the building, is absorbed by water-filled ceiling panels. It is then transferred to a heat store from which the building is heated in the winter by reversing the heat exchanging process. In this way, the ceiling panels function as heat radiators so that additional heating is not required.

Above: Stairs in living room

Opposite: East elevation by night

Below: Steel frame erection, phase 1

Below right: Living area

Bottom: Longitudinal section

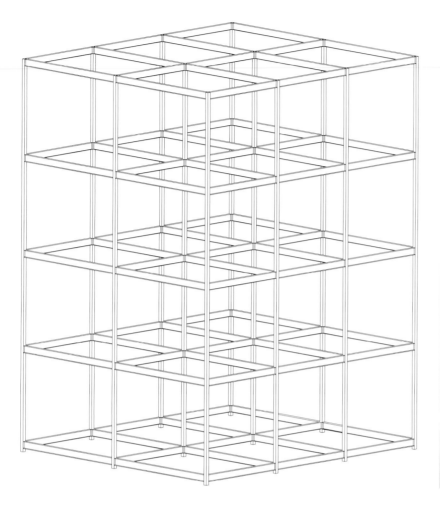

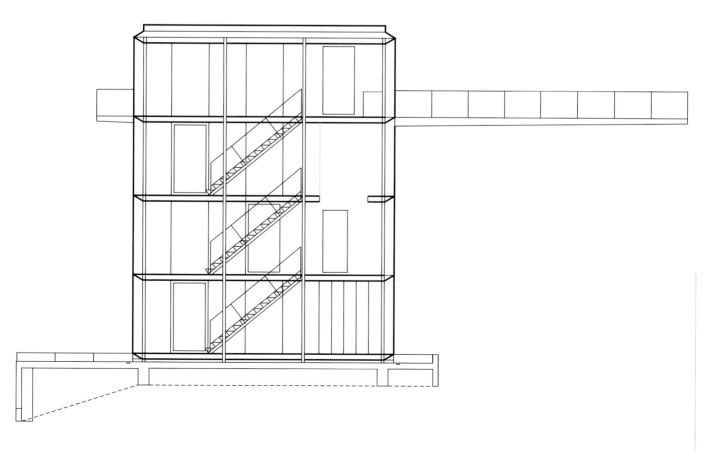

Left: Vertical access
Above: Living/dining area
Photography: Roland Halbe

Werner Sobek

Albstrasse 14
70597 Stuttgart
Germany
Telephone: +49 711 767 500
Facsimile: +49 711 767 5044
Email: mail@wsi-stuttgart.com

Werner Sobek was educated as an architect and structural engineer at the University of Stuttgart, Germany, where he also obtained his PhD in structural engineering in 1987. Having worked for Skidmore, Owings & Merrill in Chicago and for Schlaich, Bergermann & Partner in Stuttgart, he was appointed full-time professor at the University of Hannover, Germany, in 1991. In 1992, he founded his own engineering consultancy Werner Sobek Ingenieure, which has since grown to an office with 70 employees in Stuttgart, 15 in Frankfurt, and two in New York.

Werner Sobek Ingenieure is one of the leading engineering consultancies in Germany. Most notable are its special structures in glass, steel, textiles, wood, and titanium, which have received numerous awards at home and overseas. Among the consultancy's most important projects are the Ecole Nationale d'Art Décoratif in Limoges, France; the Interbank in Lima, Peru; the New Bangkok International Airport, Thailand; the Sony Center in Berlin, Germany; House R 128 in Stuttgart, Germany, as well as exhibition stands for Audi, DaimlerChrysler, BMW, and Deutsche Post.

Kallavesi Gazebo

Lake Kallavesi, Finland

Juhani Pallasmaa Architects

The Kallavesi gazebo is located on the crest of a steep rock overlooking Lake Kallavesi in eastern Finland. The landscape here, with its rocky precipices, boulders covered with lichen, pine forests and the solitary lake, evoke the famous paintings of the Finnish national romantic painters at the end of the 1800s. In this setting, the structure resembles one of the huge granite boulders, which were deposited on the site by a glacier 10,000 years ago.

The gazebo is located at the terminal point of a path, which winds around a pinnacle of rock. It is intended to be a secluded place for family meals, celebrations, and meditation in natural surroundings. The structure crops and frames the view and makes the sky an experiential element of the interior. The gazebo is a sort of 'camera obscura,' which unites the interior space and the landscape, as well as providing shelter in the great outdoors. The tiny interior is in dialogue with its surroundings to the degree that the landscape totally defines its character.

The structure is made of laminated wood frames connected and stabilized by steel parts. Laminated glass sheets hang from steel bolts. Once construction was complete, the gazebo was lifted as a complete structure to its final location by a huge crane. Fragile lichen found on the site was protected by sheets of cloth like a surgery patient in an operating room.

The gazebo was first erected on another lake's shoreline as part of a popular summer art exhibition in 2002. The exhibition enabled a rare experiment to take place where one and the same interior could be experienced and photographed in two very different settings—the photographs included here, depict both settings.

Left: Gazebo located on crest of steep rock is entered along wooden bridge through sliding doors set in inclined back wall

Photography: Rauno Träskelin

Above: View towards Lake
Kallavesi and setting sun
Photography: Rauno Träskelin

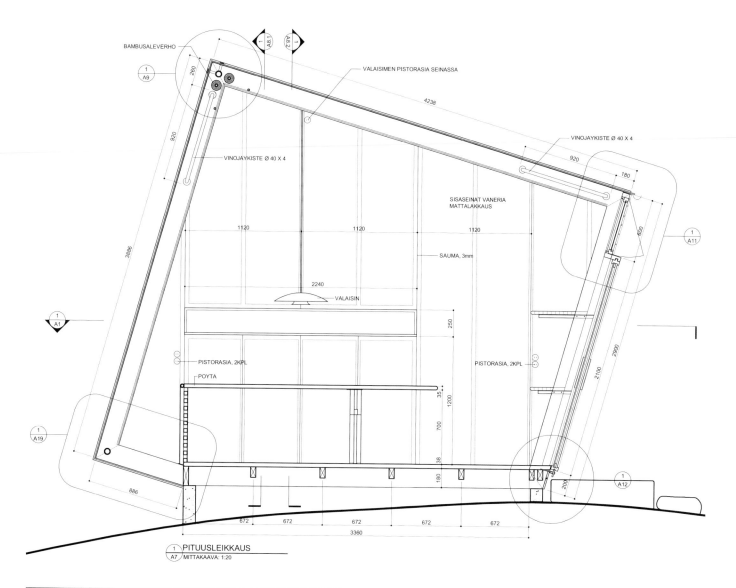

BAMBUSALEVERHO

VALAISIMEN PISTORASIA SEINASSA

4238

VINOJAYKISTE Ø 40 X 4

VINOJAYKISTE Ø 40 X 4

SISASEINAT VANERIA
MATTALAKKAUS

1120　1120　1120

SAUMA, 3mm

2240

VALAISIN

PISTORASIA, 2KPL

PISTORASIA, 2KPL

POYTA

886

672　672　672　672　672

3360

PITUUSLEIKKAUS
MITTAKAAVA: 1:20

Above: Section through gazebo. Laminated wood frame is stiffened by steel conductor units and diagonal bars

Left: Gazebo's interior at temporary location during summer art exhibition

Photography: Paavo Martikainen

Kallavesi Gazebo

243

Left: Entrance to main house

Photography: Rauno Träskelin

Juhani Pallasmaa Architects

Tehtaankaatu 13 B 28
00140 Helsinki
Finland
Telephone: +358 9 669 740
Facsimile: +358 9 669 741
Email: pallasm@clinet.fi

Having collaborated with a number of Finnish colleagues since the early 1960s, Juhani Pallasmaa, Architect SAFA, Hon. FAIA, established his own office in 1983. The firm employs 15 staff and is active in urban, architectural, product, exhibition, and graphic design.

Pallasmaa also writes and lectures extensively. He has lectured at several universities including Washington University in St. Louis, the University of Virginia, Yale University, the University of Arizona, and the Haile Selassie I University.

Pallasmaa has received awards in Finland and overseas both as an architect and a writer. His recent books include *Juhani Pallasmaa: Sensuous Minimalism*, (Beijing, 2002), *The Architecture of Image: Existential Space in Cinema* (Helsinki, 2001), *AlvarAalto: Villa Mairea 1938–39* (Helsinki, 1998) *AnimalArchitecture* (Helsinki, 1996), and *The Eyes of the Skin: Architecture and the Senses* (London, 1996).

Laminated Glasshouse
Leerdam, The Netherlands
Kruunenberg Van der Erve Architects

This monument to glass is located in Leerdam, the heart of the Dutch glass industry. The house was an initiative of the Leerdam Housing Association CWL whose brief asked competition entrants to explore new ways of using glass in construction. The Laminata House won first prize in this competition and totally redefines glass as a building material.

The project's unconventional application of glass is not only an experimental monument but also a beautiful functional residence. The Miesian quality of lightness and transparency so sought after by modernist architects has given way to a solidity and materiality seldom associated with the use of glass. A remarkable feature is the use of laminated glass sheets for external and internal walls, which vary from 3 to 56 inches thick.

The underlying design concept can best be described in the following design processes. First, a massive rectangular block is formed by laminating 2000 sheets of plate glass together. Then, the volume is sheared in its length against the grain to form two massive elements. This initial cut selectively leaves some plates intact so that the central interior spaces are created when the two elements are separated. The intact plates also serve as a reference back to the original block, as well as a reminder of the fragility of glass that contrasts with the solid laminated mass. Finally, the resulting volume is 'hollowed' out to create the other living spaces.

In reality, the construction involved pre-cutting 13,000 sheets of glass to size and then painstakingly cleaning and gluing each plate into its place on site. The resulting massive walls of laminated glass either rest on the concrete substructure that forms the basement or are suspended from the plywood roof.

The Laminated Glasshouse is a building of juxtapositions—private and translucent, robust and fragile, brittle and flexible, serene and dynamic, untamed and elegant.

Below left: Corridor looking towards toilet

Below right: Detail of structural glass element above opening between entrance hall and corridor (stainless-steel tubing incorporated into glass plates)

Above: Entrance hall

Right: Master bedroom

Laminated Glasshouse

Above: Corridor looking towards entrance

Left: View from living room towards corridor

Kruunenberg Van der Erve Architects

Conradstraat 8
NL-1056 TZ Amsterdam
The Netherlands
Telephone: +31 20 320 8486
Facsimile: +31 20 618 7550
Email: info@kvde.nl

Gerard Kruunenberg and Paul van der Erve are both graduates of the College of Advanced Technology, Faculty of Architecture, and the Academy of Architecture in Amsterdam. Having worked individually in several well-known firms both in the Netherlands and overseas, in 1996 they established Kruunenberg Van der Erve Architects.

They won an honorable mention at 'The Juice' competition for a Garden of Justice with a memorial to victims of violent crime in Los Angeles in 1995. They also won first prize in the 'Glass House' competition held in Leerdam, The Netherlands. Construction of this latter project was completed in 2001.

Lillian Way Residence

Los Angeles, California, USA

Aleks Istanbullu Architects

The client called for the architect to renovate and convert the interior of a two-bedroom house into a single-resident home. Elements of particular importance to the client included the need for closet and storage space, room for yoga practice, and accommodation for a sophisticated sound system.

The architect designed a 1200-square-foot home within the same footprint of the existing structure. Walls were removed to join spaces and to achieve more openness and light.

From the foyer, the organization of the interior is clear, with a large wall dividing the public and private sides of the house—dining room and kitchen on one side; bedroom and bath on the other. The front living area extends across the full length of the house, incorporating an open space that is reserved for the client's everyday yoga practice. The intricately articulated dividing wall includes 20-linear-feet of closet space on the bedroom side and tidy storage for the client's large classical music collection on the public side.

Although sparsely furnished, this young client is purchasing furniture carefully, including modern classics, such as a Nelson bench and three Eames stools. Working in a photo-related field, the client boasts an excellent collection of black-and-white photography. The living-room fireplace was filled in for cost reasons, resulting in an additional shelf to display photographs and beloved objects. Windows and skylights punctuate the house whenever possible to bring in natural light. Besides the front door, windowed doors to the outside are in the yoga room, kitchen, and bedroom. The backyard features a large, old tree with distinct character.

The kitchen was kept minimal and practical with plywood-facing cabinets, slate counter tops, and a slate backsplash. A movable island gives greater flexibility to the work and storage space.

Below left: Rooms are separated by partial walls to maintain openness

Below: Long storage wall divides public and private spaces

Above: Small bathroom retains open feeling with custom-designed counter and storage

Opposite: Corner storage was built to hold owner's music collection

Lillian Way Residence

Aleks Istanbullu Architects
1659 11th Street, Suite 200
Santa Monica, California, 90404
USA
Tel: +1 310 450 8246
Fax: +1 310 399 1888
Email: aistanbullu@ai-architects.com

Aleks Istanbullu Architects—established in 1986 in Santa Monica—is a creative, highly experienced firm whose work includes the master planning and design of a broad spectrum of public and private projects. Istanbullu's balanced approach to the practice of architecture instils both aesthetic and fiscal responsibility into all projects regardless of size, budget or type. His philosophy of 'strategic design' allows the firm to work in a variety of scales—from corporate to civic and educational, from multi-tenant housing to private residences—to produce an aesthetically refined, feasible, and civically responsible architecture.

Live/Work Spaces

Venice Beach, California, USA

Aleks Istanbullu Architects

When renowned architect Frank O. Gehry approached Aleks Istanbullu to work on some loft projects with him, Istanbullu was unsure where it would lead. He wondered what the architect known for elaborate, undulating forms would want from a Miesian-informed modernist, and vice versa.

A logical progression can be seen in the three projects as Istanbullu's involvement grew over time. The projects became increasingly distilled. The result in the final project—with its views of the Pacific Ocean—is the creation of pure space that is profoundly rich in shape and light.

The process of paring down the buildings to their essentials enabled Istanbullu to design economically viable spaces without loss of aesthetic richness. The result is a logic and purity that creates an effect of the sublime, as well as open and flexible spaces. Istanbullu himself has described the projects as very satisfying, because in stripping down the projects to their essentials, the design process took him to his own personal core to communicate his vision.

Throughout the lofts, concrete, plywood, glass, and open spaces define the designs. Istanbullu emphasises the importance of capturing light. Using simple materials allows the spaces to be both minimal and profound.

Below: Pure architecture is expressed in clean, light-filled space

Above: Spaces are layered with functional walls

Above right: Windows and skylights wherever possible bring in seaside light

Right: Spiral staircase leads to roof deck

Below: Upper mezzanine
houses master bedroom
and bath

Left: Kitchen is minimal
with wood island and
cabinetry
Photography: Marvin Rand

Aleks Istanbullu
1659 11th Street, Suite 200
Santa Monica, California, 90404
USA
Tel: +1 310 450 8246
Fax: +1 310 399 1888
Email: aistanbullu@ai-architects.com

Aleks Istanbullu Architects—established in 1986 in Santa Monica—is a creative, highly experienced firm whose work includes the master planning and design of a broad spectrum of public and private projects. Istanbullu's balanced approach to the practice of architecture instills both aesthetic and fiscal responsibility into all projects regardless of size, budget or type. His philosophy of 'strategic design' allows the firm to work in a variety of scales—from corporate to civic and educational, from multi-tenant housing to private residences—to produce an aesthetically refined, feasible, and civically responsible architecture.

Loft Fit-out

London, United Kingdom
Azman Owens Architects

The loft unit is situated on the top floor of a converted Victorian school with one window opening to the outside and roof-lights across the western side. The original roof trusses are still in place.

The space has a 560-square-foot footprint and two mezzanine floors, which were originally connected by a spiral staircase. Azman Owens Architects modified the mezzanines and formed an order within the space that responded to the client's brief. The third-level mezzanine was trimmed at one side and a glass floor panel was introduced along the western side, allowing daylight to filter into lower levels. Two glass floor panels were inserted into the floor and ceiling on the second-level mezzanine adjacent to the existing external window above the kitchen. One of these panels acts as the base of the bathtub, which allows natural light into the kitchen—the darkest part of the loft.

The spiral staircase was removed and a new straight staircase and shelving system were added, so that the shelving acts as the balustrade. The new staircase provides an anchor in the overall scheme, and a strong, statuesque element in the new space.

Below: Glass-bottomed bath over kitchen was particular request from client

Above: Glass floors were strategically introduced to scheme with view to introduce daylight to lower levels of loft

Right: New staircase (right) replacing too-dominant spiral has become design anchor, providing better cohesion between floors and space for shelving

Opposite: Bathroom with glass-bottomed tub and purpose-made basin cantilevering out of 'wall' of storage

Above: Detail of staircase with polished mild steel treads and risers, and uninterrupted balustrade expands between levels one and three

Photography: Keith Collie

Azman Owens Architects

18 Charlotte Road
London EC2A 3PB
United Kingdom
Telephone: +44 20 7739 8191
Facsimile: +44 20 7739 6191
Email: office@azmanowens.com

Azman Owens Architects undertake a range of projects including residential, retail, and commercial developments. Completed projects include the contemporary refurbishment of a number of listed residential buildings, new-build residential projects, and office and retail interiors.

A defined approach to new-build architecture is founded in a desire to create simple, functional, and crafted buildings. With existing buildings, the practice places value on the historic integrity of the architecture and preserves original features of value, while creating complimentary modern interventions. With design quality always at the forefront of the firm's approach, its record proves ability with successful problem solving, while maximizing and significantly improving the organization of space.

Azman Owens' work has been the subject of extensive media coverage in the UK and professional press. It was featured in a recent BBC documentary and has been nominated for RIBA Regional Awards and FX Awards for the last three consecutive years.

Malibu Residence
Malibu, California, USA
Shubin + Donaldson Architects

This project focuses on the renovation of a 1976 dwelling, including its structural reinforcement.

This beach-side modern house is perched on Malibu's Pacific Coast Highway, and features access to the beach in the back. A transitional interior entry courtyard, laid with rectangular cement pavers and bordered by smooth river rock and tufted grasses, introduces the primary design element of the home—a seamless union between interior and exterior spaces, with crisp linear architecture, ambulating plan, and visual access throughout.

The graphic grid is echoed by a geometric pattern of the cabinets and shelves that lead into the minimal kitchen. True to the open plan, the kitchen seamlessly overlooks the main living space.

The interior design palette of natural woods and limestone, white walls and fabrics, frosted and clear plate-glass creates a crisp and airy environment from which to appreciate the Pacific Ocean setting.

The ground-floor living room and adjacent sitting room offer serene respite from the sunlit terraces beyond, with cooling white and dark wood tones in the furniture and materials. Double-paned windows, which open onto the first-level terrace, permit unrestricted views onto the ocean while buffering sound (from the highway).

Openness and transformation are themes throughout the home's design and are most expressive in the master bathroom. Cool, ocean-blue frosted glass lines the walls and windows (that face another house on these sought-after lots). Behind the glass swing doors are the toilet and shower. Three layers of floor-to-ceiling glass form a translucent door that closes the space off from the bedroom, or opens it up to the master suite, porch, and Pacific Ocean beyond. Dark wenge wood—used throughout the house as an accent—encases the tub, vanity, and spacious closets. The rich brown color gently contrasts with the limestone counters and floors. Double mirrors are placed on poles in front of the frosted glass, rather than set into a wall.

Above: 'Spa-like' master bath affords views of Pacific Ocean

Above right: Mirrors are mounted to poles to allow for translucent wall behind

Malibu Residence

Opposite: There is seamless connection between outdoor patio and master bedroom

Left: Bedroom patio is surrounded by billowing fabric for shade and privacy

Below: Kitchen is center of space among living room, den, and dining room

Malibu Residence

Shubin + Donaldson Architects

3834 Willat Avenue
Culver City, California, 90232
USA
Tel: +1 310 204 0688
Fax: +1 310 204 0219
Email: rshubin@sandarc.com

Shubin + Donaldson Architects, established in 1990 in Culver City, California, is an inventive firm whose current work includes a diverse listing of commercial and residential projects ranging from entertainment-business studios, creative offices and retail stores, to community centers and custom residences. Russell Shubin, AIA, and Robin Donaldson, AIA, have distinguished principals of the 'branded environment,' which they apply to their clients in technology, advertising, Internet, and creative production. Their approach addresses the characteristics of branding, function, adaptability, and anti-hierarchical structures, which are designed with clear interior concepts and commitment to good design as a means to achieve business goals. Their residential work is context and client driven and exudes contemporary living.

Möbius

Het Gooi, The Netherlands

UN Studio

The Möbius House integrates program, circulation, and structure seamlessly. This home's design centers on a diagram of the double-locked torus, which describes two intertwining paths, tracing how two people can live together but apart, meeting at certain points that become shared spaces.

The activities of work, social life, family life, and personal time are all accommodated in the house's 'loop' structure. Movement through this loop follows the course of an active day. It is also structured by the organization of the two main materials used in the house—glass and concrete which, at points, switch places and move in front of each other. Concrete construction becomes furniture and glass façades become interior partition walls.

As a graphic representation of 24 hours of family life, the diagram acquires a time/space dimension, which leads to the implementation of a mathematical model—the Möbius band. The site and its relationship to the building are equally important to the home's overall design. The two-hectare site is divided into four areas, distinct in character. Linking these areas with the house's internal organization, the Möbius band transforms living in the house into a landscaped walk. The mathematical model of the Möbius is not literally transferred to the building but it can be found thematically in aspects of the house's design, such as lighting, the staircases, and the way in which people move through the home.

Therefore, while the Möbius diagram introduces aspects of duration and trajectory, the diagram is worked into the building in a mutated way. The implementation of this simple, borrowed drawing is the key. The two interlocking lines suggest the building's formal organization, but that is only the beginning; diagrammatic architecture is a process of unfolding and ultimately of liberation. The diagram liberates architecture from language, interpretation, and signification.

Left and right: Glass façades become interior partition walls

Above: Concrete and glass move in front of each other

Right: Concrete construction becomes furniture

Opposite: External landscape is linked into house's internal organization

Right: Interior is
transformed into
landscaped walk
Photography: Christian Richters

UN Studio
Stadhouderskade 113
1073 AX Amsterdam
The Netherlands
Telephone: +31 20 570 2040
Facsimile: +31 20 570 2041
Email: info@unstudio.com

In 1988, Van Berkel & Bos Architecture Bureau established a second practice—UN Studio. Since then Van Berkel & Bos have realized several internationally acclaimed projects including the Karbouw and ACOM office buildings, the REMU electricity station, housing projects, and the Aedes East Gallery for Kristin Feireiss in Berlin. Current projects include a music center and an electricity plant in Austria, a new town hall annex theater in Ijsselstein, and a master plan for the station area in Arnhem.

The new UN Studio is a network of specialists in architecture, urban development, and infrastructure. The firm continues with similar projects to those of Van Berkel & Bos, ranging from small- to large-scale public-network projects. However, the new firm's objective is to collaborate intensively on ambitious and influential building projects.

UN Studio is not only a design studio but, like Van Berkel & Bos, also handles the technical aspects and project supervision. However, the UN Studio does offer a new internal organization, expansion in the field of technological innovation, and a new working approach described as network practice.

Montecito Residence
Montecito, California, USA
Shubin + Donaldson Architects

A new, three-bedroom residence was built from the ground up to accommodate a substantial art collection in a restrained and economical building, and to provide accommodation for its retired owners. The site features mountain and ocean views in this decidedly upscale community.

This newly constructed residence is one of few contemporary designs in the area. It is distinctly organized with one main axis or spine that runs along the whole structure. The center of the building features the public areas with a shed roof over a long gallery for art. The open plan emphasizes space usage and contemporary living. A sculptural glass and steel fireplace separates the living area from the dining room. The far north-end block serves as the master bedroom and bathroom. The two-bedroom guest quarters are at the opposing end, and adjacent to a three-car garage. An exposed rafter system brings stability to the metal roof, while the walls of the house are plaster and glass.

Left: Industrial materials flow from inside to out

Above: Powder room has an ethereal feeling with frosted glass

Above: Kitchen includes breakfast area looking toward scenery

Right: Centrally located, kitchen shares in art collection

Top: Variety of seating areas allows for varied conversations

Left: Long hall acts as art gallery for owner's contemporary collection

Above: Entryway echoes materials and shapes of exterior entrance

Above: Open flow of space
leads from dining area to living
room, with architect-designed
fireplace in between

Photography: Tom Bonner

Shubin + Donaldson Architects

3834 Willat Avenue
Culver City, California, 90232
USA
Tel: +1 310 204 0688
Fax: +1 310 204 0219
Email: rshubin@sandarc.com

Shubin + Donaldson Architects, established in 1990 in Culver City, California, is an inventive firm whose current work includes a diverse listing of commercial and residential projects ranging from entertainment-business studios, creative offices and retail stores, to community centers and custom residences. Russell Shubin, AIA, and Robin Donaldson, AIA, have distinguished principals of the 'branded environment,' which they apply to their clients in technology,

advertising, Internet, and creative production. Their approach addresses the characteristics of branding, function, adaptability, and anti-hierarchical structures, which are designed with clear interior concepts and commitment to good design as a means to achieve business goals. Their residential work is context and client driven and exudes contemporary living.

Nomentana Residence

Lovell, Maine, USA

Mack Scogin Merrill Elam Architects

Formerly Scogin, Elam and Bray Architects

A modest site yields an intimate view across a pond to Lord's Hill, the easternmost boundary of the White Mountains National Forest. The hill, an inclined plane approaching the vertical, comforts with summer-spring greenery, dazzles with fall colors, shimmers and glistens in winter snow and ice.

The house perches at the brink of the downward slope to the pond. Breathing in the site, the house transfigures it through a series of internal spatial events—framing, focusing, enclosing, extending, dismissing, and celebrating. Relocating from the farm to the forest, the house refers to and reinterprets the 'big house, little house, back house, barn' of the famous children's rhyme.

Like Maine houses before it, this home is a result of form added onto form, spaces adjoining defensively and closely clustering, resisting long harsh Maine winters, and giving the impression of small 'house towns.' Always looking back on itself, the rooms of the house are never alone. They are rooms that are always in visual and spatial communication. The home is rural and remote but not in isolation.

Below: Living room looking towards porch

Above right: Implurium

Right: Dining room

Above left: Implurium

Top: Kitchen

Above: Guest bedroom

Below: East-west section
looking north

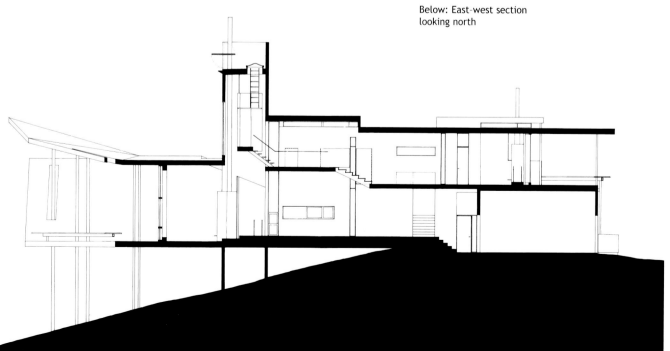

Above: Entry
Photography: Timothy Hursley

Mack Scogin Merrill Elam Architects

75 J.W. Dobbs Avenue
Atlanta, Georgia, 30303
USA
Telephone: +1 404 525 6869
Facsimile: +1 404 525 7061
Email: office@msmearch.com

Mack Scogin and Merrill Elam, the two principals of Mack Scogin Merrill Elam Architects have worked together in architecture for over 30 years. The firm, formerly known as Scogin Elam and Bray, was formed in order to take full advantage of the complimentary skills and talents of the two principals.

Projects by Mack Scogin and Merrill Elam have received over 40 design awards, including five National American Institute of Architects Awards of Excellence. Together they received the 1995 Academy Award in Architecture from the American Academy of Arts and Letters and the 1996 Chrysler Award for Innovation in Design.

Mack Scogin and Merrill Elam have had the privilege to work with some of the most prestigious and respected clients in the world. Project types include office buildings, factories, stadia, airports, health facilities, houses, dormitories, classroom and studio facilities, campus centers, libraries, museums, galleries, exhibitions, schools, warehouses, and jails, among others.

Current and recent projects include the Wang Campus Center and Davis Garage for Wellesley College in Massachusetts; the United States Federal Courthouse in Austin, Texas; a School of Architecture for The Ohio State University in Columbus, Ohio; a Music Library for The University of California at Berkeley in California, and the Herman Miller Cherokee Operations facility in Canton, Georgia.

O'Neil Guesthouse

West Los Angeles, California, USA

Lubowicki Lanier Architecture

The O'Neill guesthouse is 800 square feet in area and consists of two major elements—a bedroom and a living room separated by an earthen stair. Similar to a bunker, the bedroom is partially buried in the ground and has a suspended roof form in the shape of a boat, planted with wild grass. The living room is copper-sheeted on the exterior with maple panels on the interior, reminiscent of an old crate. Strips of glass separate each panel to further accentuate the design and to break down the scale.

The earthen stair connects the upper pool deck and the lower garden, and allows the landscape to 'join' the rooms together. The dining table is set beneath the stair, while behind all three forms and underneath the pool deck are located the kitchen, bathroom, and service areas, which connect the rooms. The roof of this area is level with the pool and constructed from broken concrete set in sod, bringing the lower garden up to the pool deck.

Below: Living

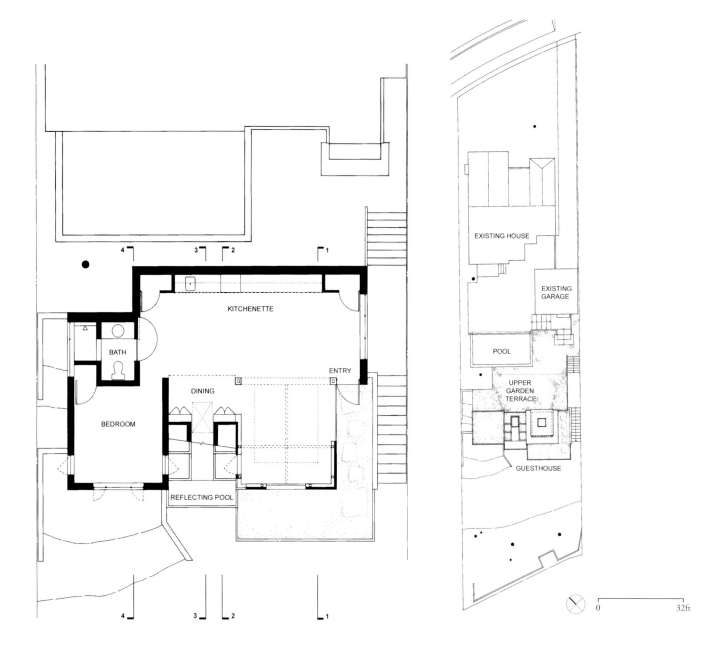

KITCHENETTE

BATH

ENTRY

DINING

BEDROOM

REFLECTING POOL

4 3 2 1

EXISTING HOUSE

EXISTING GARAGE

POOL

UPPER GARDEN TERRACE

GUESTHOUSE

0   32ft

Above left: Floor plan

Above right: Site plan

Right: Bedroom

Above: Entry, living, and dining

Left: Living and dining

Above left: Bedroom

Above right: Living

Photographer: Erich Koyama

Lubowicki Lanier Architecture

141 Sierra Street
El Segundo, California, 90245
USA
Telephone: +1 310 322 0211
Facsimile: +1 310 322 3620
Email: info@lubowickilanier.com

In 1998, Paul Lubowicki and Susan Lanier established the architectural firm of Lubowicki Lanier Architecture. Recently, their practice was selected as one of the 'LA 12,' representing the third generation of influential architects in Los Angeles. Lubowicki Lanier has designed several award-winning residential and commercial projects, and the firm's work has been published widely in international and local publications.

Lubowicki Lanier approach the design of each project as an opportunity to bring together in the program the unique characteristics of site, context, and client. These principals combine into a dynamic set of relationships that find expression architecturally. Attention to such principals is what makes the practice of architecture an art. Each building reveals the creation of a common language integrating these relationships.

Perry Street Loft

Greenwich Village, New York, USA

Hariri & Hariri — Architecture

This project was developed conceptually as a temple for art, a sanctuary for the soul and a refuge for the body.

Architecturally the whole space is organised around LIGHT. One enters the apartment on the upper level. Upon arrival, a light-wall greets the visitor and becomes the center of the apartment. This physical and spiritual center is a backdrop for the owner's collection as well as being a vertical connector between the two floors, organising the space and circulation while providing illumination for both floors.

The space on both floors is continuous from the street to the garden allowing natural light to penetrate and filter throughout the apartment. All the wet elements such as the kitchen, shower and powder room are along the east wall and are behind translucent screens on tracks. These screens conceal the spaces behind while allowing light in.

At the end, a double-story sanctuary filled with light, enclosed by a curtain wall, opening into the garden becomes a space where one is both inside and outside at once. Here space, light, water, fire, and earth, blur the boundary between the material & spiritual world.

Left: Living area with sculpted fireplace wall

Above: Living area opens
into garden allowing one
to be inside and outside at
once

Right: Guest bathroom
with tribal wooden
cabinetry and Native-
American carved-stone
sink

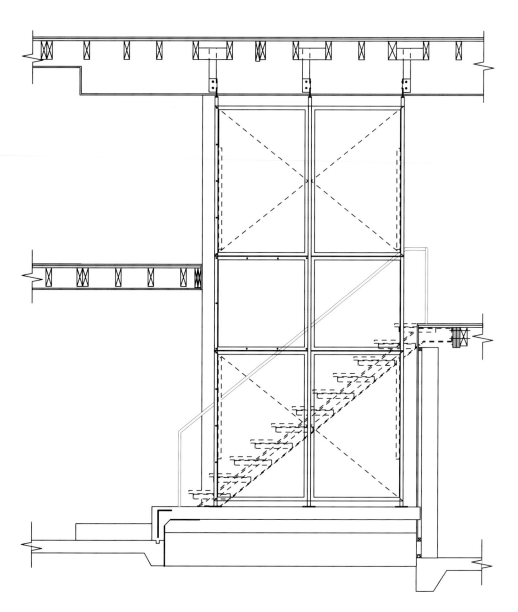

Left: Drawing of light wall and stair connecting two levels

Below left: Double-story sanctuary with light wall and stair

Below right: Water trough continues from inside to outside blurring boundary between material and spiritual world

Perry Street Loft

Above: Sculpted fireplace wall

Photography: Paul Warchol

Hariri & Hariri - Architecture

18 East 12th Street #1C
New York, NY 10003
Telephone: +1 212 727 0338
Facsimile: +1 212 727 0479
email: info@haririandhariri.com

Hariri & Hariri was established in 1986 by Gisue Hariri and Mojgan Hariri. The two partners began their architectural collaboration very early on while still students at Cornell, working together on various competitions and theoretical projects. After graduation from Cornell University and completion of their apprenticeship with distinguished architectural offices, the Iranian born sisters set up their private practice in New York City, dedicated to research and construction of Innovative ideas.

Steinhauser Boathouse
Fussach, In der Schanz, Austria

Marte.Marte

The Steinhauser Boathouse in Fussach is situated amid an 'El Dorado' of informal improvised buildings. Roof pitch, height, and distance from the site boundaries are the only council stipulations; everything else is subject to a game of improvisation. Marte.Marte's boathouse adopts this 'game' with the irregular rhythm on its façade and the changing pattern of rivets. However, it also stands out from neighboring buildings by playing by different rules.

The starting point for the boathouse's design is abstract rather than ecstatic romanticism—a form with openings that only by chance resembles a house. The boathouse's timber structure with a closed aluminum façade rests on an extended concrete retaining wall at the water's edge. A 21-foot-wide sliding door indicates the protected approach to the double-story boat garage. Living and sleeping areas are located on the second floor.

The sleeping area is compact, organized as an introverted core that retreats behind the closed-up façade. Narrow viewing slits in the façade provide light and orientation. On the building's exterior, a band of narrow perforations runs below these openings, behind which are located ventilation flaps for the bedrooms.

Roof access requires the use of hydraulics. At the press of a switch, a staircase folds out from the ceiling. With the design of this staircase, Marte.Marte introduced aspects of the client's occupation (a vehicle-part manufacturer) into the design. Loading flaps, coachwork technology and aluminum provide the references.

Left: Hydraulically operated staircase, side view

Left: Dining

Below left: Plan

Below: Staircase

Opposite: Hallway to sleeping births

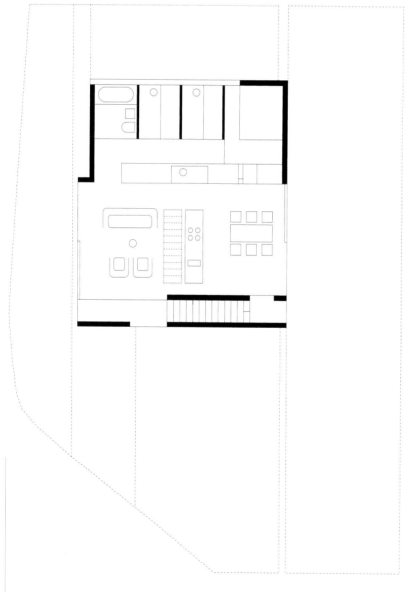

Steinhauser Boathouse

Left: Fireplace
Phototgraphy: Albrecht
Imanuel Schnabel

Marte.Marte

Totengasse 18
6833 Weiler
Vorarlberg, Austria
Telephone: +43 5523 52587
Facsimile: +43 5523 525879
Email: architekten@marte-marte.com

The office of Marte.Marte was founded in 1993. The practice's objective is to realize complex architectural requirements in as clear structures as possible. In doing so its work follows the sentiment of a quote from the late-German architect Heinrich von Tessenow, 'das Einfache ist nicht immer das Beste, aber das Beste ist immer einfach' ('what is simple is not always the best, but the best is always simple').

Marte.Marte has designed domestic housing and various public buildings, including Beschützende Werkstätte der Caritas (a workshop for people with disabilities) in Bludenz, completed 2002; the System Industrie Electronic AG company in Lustenau, Austria; Frödisch Bridge in Muntlix, completed 1999, and Totenkapelle (a chapel) in Weiler, completed 1994. For Marte.Marte's Cemetery in Batschuns project, the firm received the Österreichischer Bauherrenpreis 2002, (an Austrian Award for Architecture).

T House

Paris, France

Jakob+MacFarlane Architects

The T House project involved adding a further floor to the initial extension of the dwelling built in 1984. The additional floor comprises a 431-square-foot loft space for the owner's children. A decision was made to design this floor with a different identity to the rest of the house, in order to set it apart as a separate functional identity within the overall design of the home.

The completed project resulted in the creation of two igloo-type volumes constructed from zinc, perched on the roof of the existing house. These volumes are broken up into several smaller volumes, taking into account the dictates imposed by the various views from the roof. The volumes dovetail to create a series of openings with complex geometric forms, offering views skyward and toward the street.

Below: View of interior towards street

Above: View towards entry
stairs

Right: Section

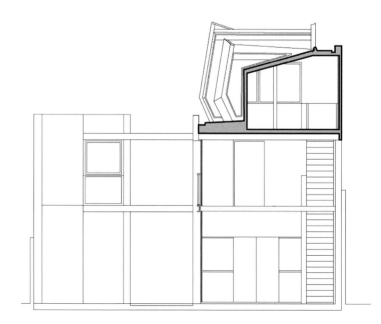

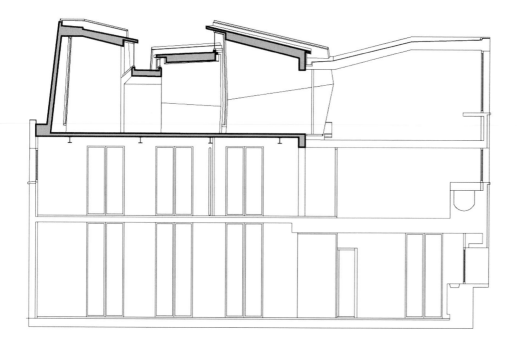

Above: Longitudinal
section

Left: Detail of pleat
opening

Above: View towards roof
opening
Photography: Nicolas Borel

Jakob+MacFarlane Architects
13–15 Rue Des Petites Ecuries
75010 Paris
France
Telephone: +33 1 4479 0572
Facsimile: +33 1 4800 9793
Email: jakmak@club-internet.fr

Jakob+Macfarlane is a French architectural studio based in Paris, France. Dominique Jakob completed his architectural studies at the l'Ecole d'Architecture Paris-Villemin/Malaquais. Brendan Macfarlane studied at the Southern Californian Institute of Architecture (Sci-Arch) in Los Angeles and the Harvard Graduate School of Design. They established their practice in 1992, while teaching at the Special Architecture School in Paris-Nare.

Jakob and Macfarlane have completed a number of projects across France, including the award-winning entry for the restaurant refurbishment at the top of the George Pompidou Centre in Paris in 2000. They have lectured as visiting professors in architecture schools across Europe including the Berlage Institute in Amsterdam, the Bartlett School of Architecture in London and the l'Ecole Spéciale d'Architecture in Paris. their work has been exhibited at the Max Protech Gallery in New York, Archilab in Orleans, France, the George Pompidou Centre in Paris, in the American and French Pavilion at the Biennale of Architecture in Venice, and the Victoria and Albert Museum in London.

Teng House

Singapore

SCDA Architects Pte.Ltd.

The suburbs of Singapore have been highly urbanized due to changes in zoning regulations. The Teng House is located on a tight suburban lot where plot ratios have been intensified and the height allowance increased to three floors. In this project's case, the neighboring house is less than 12 feet away, making privacy a key concern.

The house is conceived as a latticed, two-story wooden box, entirely constructed from steel and timber, suspended above ground level. A sheer wall has been built 3 feet from the building on the side facing a neighboring house, which acts as a privacy barrier. This 3-foot slot allows light to wash against the sheer wall, reflecting it back toward the house. All the plumbing and services are organized in a zone to the right of the partition wall.

The façades are designed with a double skin. Fixed timber louvers are angled down to allow for outside views, while maintaining privacy at street level. The façade's glazing also has operable panels for natural ventilation. Only at ground level are the windows visually unobstructed to ensure views of the narrow garden between the two houses.

The living area is well supplied with natural light from above and to the side, and white walls further enhance illumination in this area. Floor-to-ceiling windows have been fitted with fixed, external wooden louvers to ensure privacy.

Below: Heart of living space is sunken conversation pit. Beyond, timber footbridge spans pool, and open riser staircase ascends to second-story

Photography: Jacob Termansen

Opposite: Centilevered stair treads lead to steel and glass bridge that spans central lightwell and connects two bedrooms at second story

Photography: Jacob Termansen

Left: Details of master bathroom and dressing room

Photography: Jacob Termansen

Below left: Steel and glass bridge spanning central lightwell connecting two bedrooms at second story

Below: Small palm court contributes to overwhelming sense of calmness in internalised world

Photography: Peter Mealin

Teng House

Above: Master bedroom at third-story level. Owner prefers simple mattress on timber floor. Box spring is sunken into timber platform floor

Photography: Peter Mealin

SCDA Architects Pte. Ltd.

10 Teck Lim Road
Singapore 088386
Singapore
Telephone: +65 6324 5458
Facsimile: +65 6324 5450
Email: scda@starhub.net.sg

SCDA Architects is a multidisciplinary architectural practice established in 1995. The design principal is a graduate from Yale University and has extensive professional and academic experience, having taught in universities in the United States and Singapore. The office currently employs 32 staff, 21 of whom are architects, three interior designers and one graphic designer. The practice's holistic approach to architecture includes full interior design and planning services. The firm also has broad experience with private residences, resort hotels, apartments, and commercial buildings.

Two Houses

Furulund, Oslo, Norway

Lund Hagem Architects

Retaining all 25 mature trees on the 12,500-square-foot site was essential to planning the design of two L-shaped houses at Furulund. The houses are positioned in relation to each other along the wall that divides them.

In house A, the central staircase leads up to a double-height study with a mezzanine floor, before reaching a roof terrace. The parent's area is also located at the top of the stairs and has access to the study's mezzanine floor. Half a level down, the children's area has direct access to a sheltered atrium. Across the living area, kitchen, and terrace areas, an expansive roof light is used to illuminate the space. At the end wall in this area, a fireplace dominates.

House B is organized around a garden-level corridor. The master bedroom, family area with kitchen and dining, and the sitting room all open off this corridor. The children's area is half a level up and a narrow staircase leads to the roof terrace.

The houses are constructed from lightweight concrete block, rendered on both sides. The lighter volumes are panelled in untreated oak, while the floors are of polished concrete interspersed with polished wood (ash).

Below: View toward garden

Photography: Svein Lund

Left: Living/patio

Below: Studio terrace

Bottom: Entrance façade

Photography: Gronli (left); Svein Lund (below, bottom)

Two Houses

Left: Main entrance with view through studio

Photography: Gronli

Lund Hagem Architects

Wergelandsveien 25
0167 Oslo
Norway
Telephone: +47 2333 3150
Facsimile: +47 2269 8578
Email: mail@lundhagem.no

Lund Arkitekter MNAL was established in 1984. In 1990 the office changed its name to Lund Hagem Arkitekter AS. At the same time a second office was established in Sandefjord, Norway. The firm's partners are Svein Lund and Einar Hagem, employing 24 additional staff.

The practice's architectural vision is based on its interpretation of each specific site's landscape. With this vision, the firm seeks to form a modern and timeless architecture with its roots in Norwegian tradition. Lund Hagem Arkitekter AS has comprehensive experience in urban planning, multi-dwelling housing, detached houses and summerhouses, as well as retirement homes, office buildings, museums, and a university campus. Lund Hagem Architects has won several national architectural awards.

Underground Swimming Pool
Vienna, Austria

The next ENTERprise – architects

The swimming pool is accessed through the basement of an imposing late 19th-century house. The pool is located at the far end of the garden beyond the shade cast by the house. After a short walk leading gently downwards, the narrow corridor opens into a light-flooded landscape. On arrival to this separate indoor pool area, visitors are left with the sense of being in some parallel universe, removed from the house and its immediate surroundings.

Colors and materials used to furnish this space are reminiscent of both a living room and ocean travel, and mahogany is used generously. However, the indoor pool area remains elusive, so visitors must draw their own conclusions about the other functions of this space, which also includes a sauna, solarium, and kitchen. The many projections, moldings, openings, and screens do not immediately reveal these functions. The swimming pool itself, is akin to an oversized bathtub, partly freestanding in the imaginative space it accommodates.

Below: Pool deck

Right: Daylight penetrates interior

Below left: View of ascent from pool area to garden

Below right: section

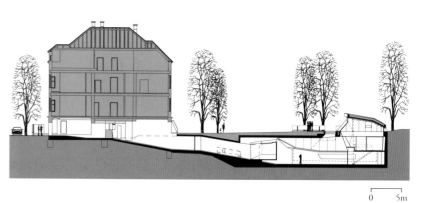

0   5m

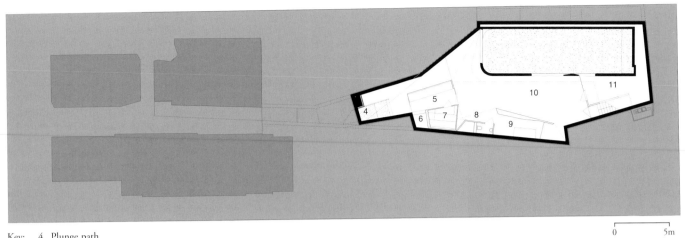

Key: 4 Plunge path
      5 Rest area
      6 Shower
      7 Sauna
      8 Kitchen
      9 Solarium
     10 Fitness or living area
     11 Technical support

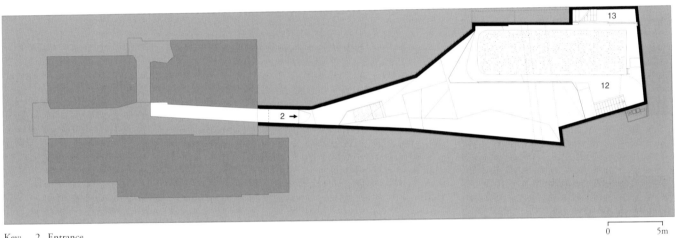

Key: 2 Entrance
     12 Pool
     13 Atrium (exit garden)

Top: Ground-level floor plan 5-meters below basement level

Middle: Ground-level floor plan 2-meters below basement level

Left: View back toward ramp and sauna

Underground Swimming Pool

Above: Ascent to pool area
Photography: Gerald Zugmann

The next ENTERprise – architects
ernst j. fuchs | marie-therese harnoncourt
Ausstellungsstrasse 5/13
A-1020 Vienna
Austria
Telephone: +43 1 729 6388
Facsimile: +43 1 729 6752
Email: mth.harnoncourt@sil.at

In 2000, Ernst J. Fuchs and Marie Therese Harnoncourt founded The next ENTERprise architecture office in Vienna. They both graduated from the University of Applied Arts in Vienna and have been working together since the early 1990s, mainly in collaboration with Florian Haydn under the professional name of POOR BOYsENTERPRISE. Since 1997, Fuchs and Harnoncourt have taught at the University of Applied Arts Vienna , the Technical University of Vienna and Innsbruck, and others. They are co-authors of *Urban Interventions* (Hirnsegel Nr.7 1995, Stadtwind 2000), *Experimental Installations* (Blindgänger 2000, Audiolounge 2002), *Architectual Work* (House Zirl 1997, Underground Pool 2001, Puplic Lackbaths Kaltern 2002) and *Urban Concepts* (How to Start a City 2003).

Gil Fashion Area 1
Vienna, Austria

propeller z

The spatial concept of the store conversion can easily be read through the transparent façade. The façade consists of a system of intersecting planes: lime-green vertical and gray horizontal extrusions that open up to the street, while covering and simplifying the irregular and cramped spaces of the existing 1920s structure. The protruding ground floor façade reaches out vertically, partly overlapping the large patterned glass area of the upper floor.

A thin steel 'hairpin' draws the overlying weight of the building downward with ease and a delicate 'floating' staircase leads to the sales area on the upper floor. On this floor in the two flanking main spaces, the floors and the walls—both made out of warm-gray linoleum—merge gradually and extend up to the ceiling.

The two main spaces are connected via corridors whose walls have been expanded through the insertion of recesses from high-gloss prefabricated polyester units, which can be used for laying out products for display. The changing cubicles are located at either end of the corridors, which are also constructed of industrial prefabricated polyester units.

Below: Both levels visually connected by gallery-like double-height space

Above: Street level—stairs with mesh-filled stainless-steel railings

Left: Painted MDF wall claddings in corridors with backlit recesses for display purposes

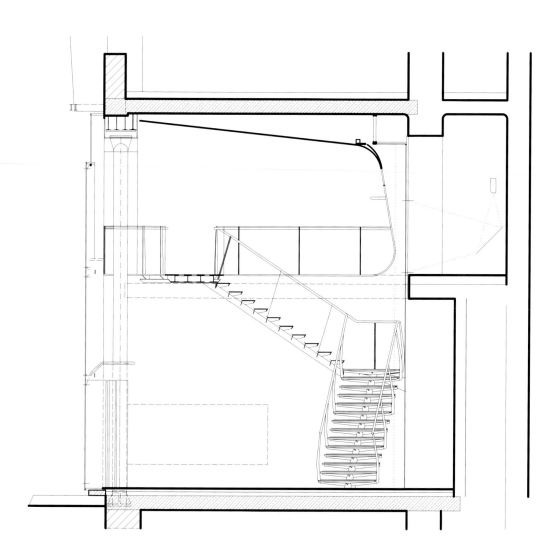

Gil Fashion Area 1

Left: Changing room from
prefab polyester units

Below: Retail space upper
level

Photography: Margherita Spiluttini

propeller z
Mariahilferstrasse 101/3/55
A-1060 Vienna
Austria
Telephone: +43 1 595 2727 0
Facsimile: +43 1 595 2727 27
Email: mail@propellerz.at

Since 1994, the propeller z team has produced work in the fields of architecture, interior design, exhibition/set design, graphic design, and experimental work. By means of non-linear analytical processes, propeller z try to reveal, sharpen, and formulate solutions, which already feature in a given brief.

Propeller z's work is about performing a balancing act in a web composed of functional, programmatic, and financial constraints, coupled with the individual interests of each team member involved. Continuous discourse throughout a project's development ensures that each design decision remains a source of discussion, and the proportionality of the means is constantly monitored. This also consciously prevents the creation of a recurring style.

Giorgio Armani Store
Milan, Italy

Claudio Silvestrin Architects

Following the commission to design the Giorgio Armani boutique in Place Vendôme in Paris, Claudio Silvestrin was asked to design all of the Giorgio Armani stores worldwide. With the refurbishment of the Paris store, design refurbishment was undertaken for the stores in Europe (such as Milan, Moscow, and London), America (such as Boston and Chicago), and Asia (such as Dubai, Tokyo, and Hong Kong). Newly built stores in São Paulo and Seoul provided an opportunity to extend the timeless and elegant image created for Giorgio Armani to entire buildings.

Silvestrin describes the store as possessing a style that transcends minimalism and strives for timeless elegance. One of the boutique's distinguishing features is a dramatic 150-foot-long perspective view of its interior double-height space. This can be seen through the window from outside the store or from the top of the stairs inside.

The store's walls and floor are constructed from raw French limestone and the furniture, designed by Silvestrin, was crafted from Macassar ebony.

Below: Interior of store

Above: Ramp

Right: Entrance

Giorgio Armani Store

Left: Ramp with staircase beyond

Below: Ramp

Bottom left: Long corridor with ebony display bench

Left: Store interior
Photo credit: Matteo Piazza

Claudio Silvestrin Architects

Unit 18 Waterside
44–48 Wharf Road
London N1 7UX
United Kingdom
Telephone: +44 207 490 7797
Facsimile: +44 207 490 7272
Email: c.silvestrin@claudiosilvestrin.com

Born in 1954, Claudio Silvestrin was trained in Milan by AG Fronzoni and studied at the Architectural Association in London. He practices worldwide from his London office, established in 1989.

Silvestrin's work includes day-to-day structures, domestic and commercial interiors, public galleries, and houses. Clients include Giorgio Armani, illycaffé, Anish Kapoor, Calvin Klein, Cappellini, and the Fondazione Sandretto Re Rebaudengo for whom he has designed a newly built museum in Turin. Silvestrin's works and writing are published in the book entitled *Claudio Silvestrin* (Birkhauser).

Silvestrin's integrity, clarity of mind, inventiveness, and attention to detail is reflected in his rigorous minimal architecture: austere but not extreme, contemporary yet timeless, calming but not ascetic, strong but not intimidating, elegant but not ostentatious.

Hermes Store

Tokyo, Japan

Renzo Piano Building Workshop

In collaboration with Rena Dumas Architecture Intérieure (Paris)

French fashion group Hermès chose the Ginza district in central Tokyo for its Japanese headquarters—a 54,000-square-foot building comprising shopping space, workshops, offices, exhibition and multimedia areas, topped by a French-style hanging garden.

The project presented both aesthetic and technical challenges. Given Tokyo's architectural diversity, and Japan's strict building practices to counter seismic activity, how to create a major landmark building was a design issue. The design solution was a 'magic lantern' lighting up Ginza, like lanterns traditionally hung above the doors of Japanese houses.

The building's façades are made of 15- x 15-inch glass blocks especially designed and manufactured for the project. The glass-block façades create a continuous and luminous screen between the serenity of the inner spaces and the activity of the surrounding city.

The building was constructed using a steel structural system that is articulated at strategic locations with visco-elastic dampers, from which cantilevered floors span to support the suspended glass-block façades.

At the building's center, a small open square connects the street to the subway two levels below, via an escalator. Susumu Shingu's mobile sculpture overlooks the space, engaging a continuous play of light between the façade, the city, and the sky.

Left: Showroom designed by Rena Dumas Architecture Intérieure

Left: 10th-floor meeting room beside terrace

Below: Area on floor with large reflecting pools set in floor. Sculpture by Susumu Shingu

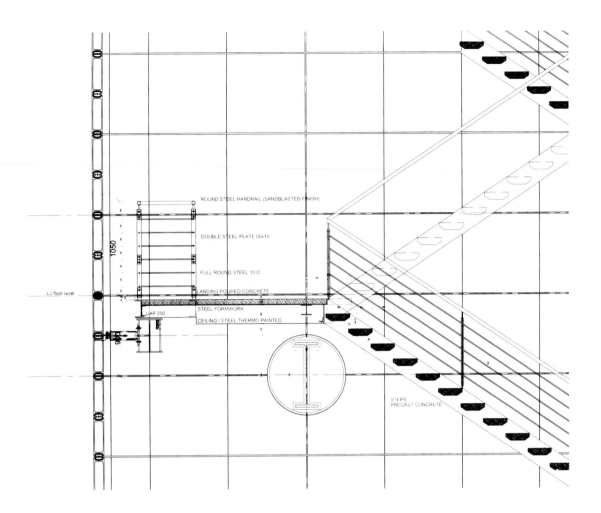

ROUND STEEL HANDRAIL (SANDBLASTED FINISH)

DOUBLE STEEL PLATE 50x10

FULL ROUND STEEL 10 O

1050

LANDING POURED CONCRETE

L3 floor level

STEEL FORMWORK

UAP 250

CEILING / STEEL THERMO PAINTED

STEPS
PRECAST CONCRETE

Top: Vertical section.
Details of staircase and
attachment of glass facing

Above: Entrance zone

Left: Glass facing

Renzo Piano Building Workshop

via P.P. Rubens 29
16158 Genova
Italy
Telephone: +39 10 61711
Facsimile: +39 10 6171350
Email: renzopianobwit@bwge.it

Renzo Piano was born in Italy in 1937. He graduated from the Milan Polytechnic School of Architecture in 1964. As a student, he worked under the guidance of Franco Albini, while regularly attending his father's building sites where he gained invaluable practical experience. Between 1965 and 1970 he undertook study trips to Britain and America and completed a number of formal experiments.

In 1971, he founded the Piano & Rogers agency with Richard Rogers, his partner on the Centre Pompidou project in Paris. In 1977, he founded l'Atelier Piano & Rice with engineer Peter Rice, a professional personality who would work with him on many projects until his death in 1993. He then founded Renzo Piano Building Workshop, which has offices in Paris and Genoa.

Miss Sargfabrik

Vienna, Austria

BKK-3

MISS is a project aimed at satisfying the hybrid needs of the 21st-century urban human being: living spaces, working spaces, possibilities for dreaming, and common spaces make up this project. The design intent was to banish from traditional workspaces loneliness and loss of individuality and community. These notions are no longer in opposition to one another or misplace each other; instead their collective juxtaposition provides new challenges for architecture.

In this prototypical project, BKK-3 has attempted to unify multiple 'layers' of an idea, which until now have been considered incompatible with one another in the program and design of social housing. BKK-3's concept was to create a piece of evolutionary architecture, to create space for development. Some of the project's roots are to be found in the exemplary tradition of Viennese social housing, while others take up communitarian ideas as realized in the firm's previous project 'Sargfabrik,' which integrates culture and housing.

Above: City looks at you

Above: Landscape and space floats into rooms

Above right: Always nearer heaven

Right: Light-emitting interface

Above: Minute rush
Photography: Hertha Hurnaus

BKK-3
Missindorfstrasse 10/4
1140 Vienna
Austria
Telephone: +43 1 7869 3930
Facsimile: +43 1 7869 39393
Email: mail@bkk-3.com

BKK-3 is a Viennese architecture studio modeled on the workings of a collective enterprise. The studio consists of two principle architects, Johan Winter and Franz Sumnitsch, and a group of 16 associated architects and other staff. Projects to date include a library building in Upper Austria, a mixed-use home-office space in Vienna, commercial buildings, a stadium in Salzburg and an Expo pavilion in Biel.

The office has won a number of prizes, including the prestigious Adolf Loos Prize for Architecture for their Sargfabrik project. Their work has been exhibited in several architectural exhibitions in Austria, as well as having received extensive press coverage in both print and radio at home and overseas.

Prada
New York, New York, USA
OMA

The New York Prada store project is an interior conversion of the former Guggenheim store in Soho. The 23,000-square-foot project covers the ground floor and basement of the building. In order to connect the ground floor and basement areas smoothly, and guide customers to the more obscure parts of the store, the floor steps downward across its entire width. It then rises to reconnect with the ground floor, creating a large 'wave.'

The oversized wave stair, made of zebrawood, is used as an informal display space, where people can try on shoes and browse through bags and other accessories. At the push of a button, an event platform rotates out of the opposite part of the wave, turning the stair into an auditorium for performances, film projections, and lectures. Large metal cages for merchandise and display are suspended from an overhead track system, resembling inverted buildings in a street—a 'hanging city.' These display volumes can contract at the back of the store into a solid volume and free up the floor space for public activities.

Below: Round glass elevator and wallpaper mural

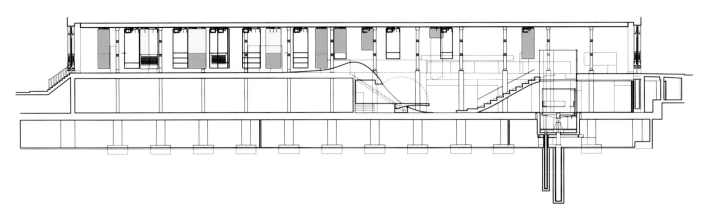

Top left: Event platform

Top right: Round glass elevator and wallpaper mural

Middle: Section

Above: 'Hanging City'

Right: 'Triptych' plasma screens

Above left: Retail display stair

Right: Retail space

OMA

Heer Bokelweg 149
NL 3032 AD Rotterdam
The Netherlands
Telephone: +31 10 243 8200
Facsimile: +31 10 243 8202
Email: office@oma.nl

The Office for Metropolitan Architecture (OMA) is a Rotterdam-based firm concerned with contemporary architecture, urbanism, and general cultural issues. Established in 1975, the office employs 100 architects and designers of multinational origin. Architects, designers, CAD-architects, model makers, and graphic designers work in close collaboration. Expert consultants on relevant issues are involved from the beginning of the design process.

Since the firm's inception, OMA has realised several projects, ranging from private residences to large-scale urban planning. Currently, OMA is engaged in its largest project to date: the new headquarters for the China Central Television (CCTV), a 6,189,000-square-foot headquarters and cultural center in Beijing, to be completed in 2008 for the Olympic Games.

Selfridges Technology Hall
London, UK

Ron Arad Associates

Selfridges department store in London's Oxford Street, unveiled its new Technology Hall in November 2001. The space is designed as a fashionable, funky environment on the lower ground floor of the store, specifically aimed at technology retailing. The futuristic, high-tech, and interactive showcase serves as a virtual open space for adults. The 21,530-square-foot space is designed to showcase and retail well-known brand names and concessions in technology products. The new environment has been specifically designed to enhance the customer experience of technology products through design-driven branding of both the products and the retail space they occupy.

Below: Photographic retail concession

Below Right: Laptop display wall

Bottom: Detail of canopy display case

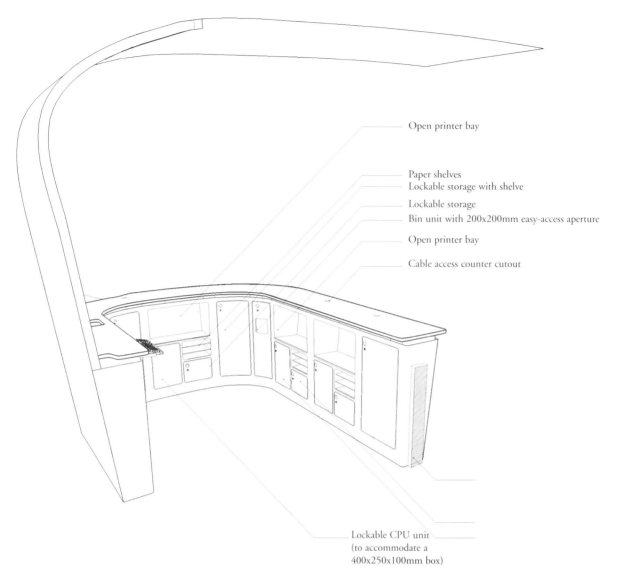

Open printer bay

Paper shelves
Lockable storage with shelve

Lockable storage
Bin unit with 200x200mm easy-access aperture

Open printer bay

Cable access counter cutout

Lockable CPU unit
(to accommodate a
400x250x100mm box)

Above: 3D image of
canopy retail counter

Right: View of canopy into
sound and vision
concession

Left: Sony display wall

Below: Detail of photographic wall camera display mounts

Photography: Ron Arad Associates Ltd

Ron Arad Associates
62 Chalk Farm Road
London
United Kingdom
Telephone: +44 207 284 4963
Facsimile: +44 207 379 0499
Email: info@ronarad.com

Educated in Israel, Ron Arad moved to the United Kingdom in 1973 to study architecture at the prestigious Architectural Association, London. In 1981, he established One Off Ltd with Caroline Thorman, a design studio, workshop, and showroom located in Covent Garden. Ron Arad Associates was formed in 1989, specializing in architectural projects, installations, furniture, and industrial design. Since 1994 Ron Arad has taught in a number of professorial positions at universities across Europe, he is currently Professor of Design Product at the Royal College of Art in London.

Space Concepts
Interior Design Show, Toronto, Canada
II BY IV Design Associates Inc.

One visitor to Toronto's Interior Design Show described the futuristic living space exhibit 'Space Concepts,' designed by II BY IV Design Associates, as 'Buckminster Fuller meets Tom Ford.' In it, the designers created a magical interpretation of a futuristic lifestyle, in a minimalist, unconventional, and theatrical setting.

When the show organizers invited II BY IV to create a living space exhibit to influence and inspire design consumers and professionals alike, the firm drew on two inspirations. The first was the idea of creating a viable human resort on the moon constructed from existing Spacelab structural modules. The other inspiration drew on II BY IV's pre-existing work in the conversion of warehouse and office buildings to hotels, and the creation of mixed-use projects.

The provocative result of the designers' musings about the future of the travel and accommodation industry turned out to be the show's runaway hit. Pulsating with the beat of a relentlessly compelling dance mix, the multipurpose, dramatically lit, white-on-white interior they created, inside a lightweight geodesic dome, was unexpectedly snug and inviting.

Could the project be described as an efficiency unit for a space traveler? Perhaps a sophisticated and highly functional extended-stay suite, or an easily assembled, shipped and installed prefabricated package for building retrofits. Fantastic and futuristic perhaps, but nonetheless demonstrating a set of practical construction techniques, materials, finishes, and details for today's developers, not just tomorrow's.

Below: Futuristic living room is inviting and provocative

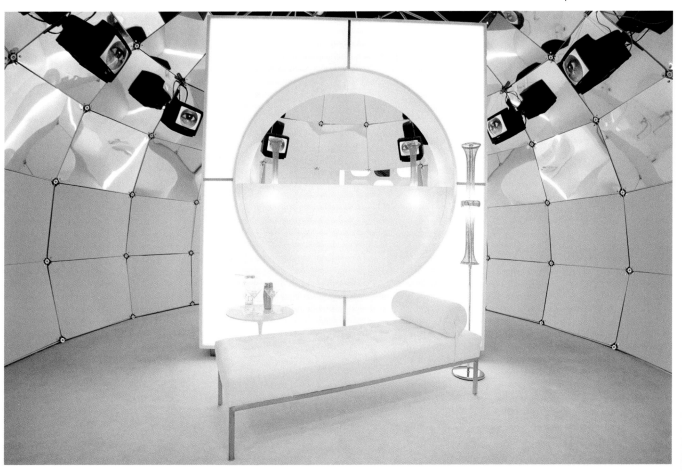

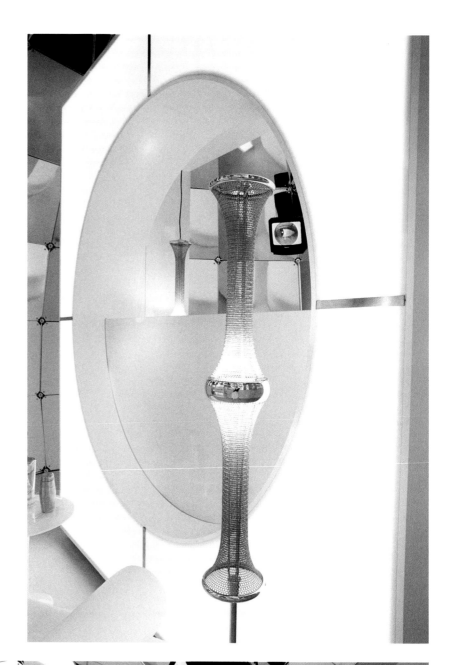

Right: Porthole both reveals and conceals rear sleep area

Below: Tidy plug-in dressing module includes generous storage

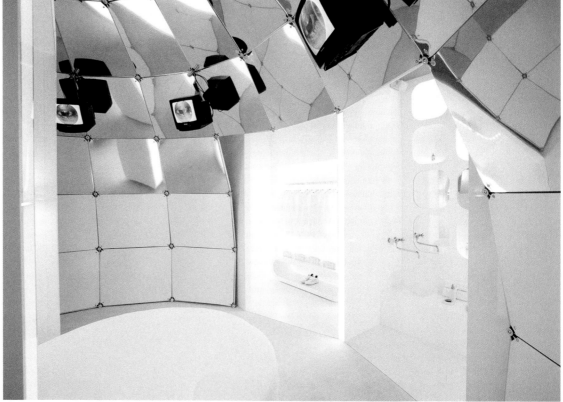

Below: Sleek and compact kitchen module is highly organized

Bottom: Carefully detailed bathing module is elegant and efficient

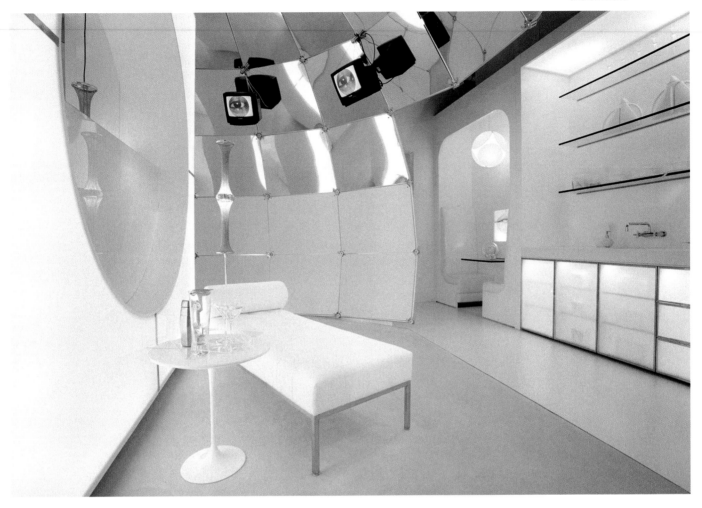

Above left: Backlighting equally flatters hanging clothes and their owner

Above right: Video screen replaces jukebox in ultra-modern dining module

Photography: David Whittaker

II BY IV Design Associates Inc.
77 Mowat Avenue, Suite 109
Toronto, ON M6K 3E3
Canada
Telephone: +1 416 531 2224
Facsimile: +1 416 642 0102
Email: design@iibyiv.com

II BY IV Design Associates is committed to 'designing magically, thinking practically.' The firm has won more than 70 awards for interior design and lighting design internationally, and the company's founders have been declared 'Designers of the Year' three times. II BY IV was named one of the 'Top 50 International Firms' by the magazine *Visual Merchandising and Store Design* and received 'Best of Show' at the 21st Annual Gold Key Awards for Excellence in Hospitality Design.

II BY IV has touched every aspect of daily life. Their expert interpretation of current and emerging consumer lifestyles, attitudes, and expectations is demonstrated in the design of extraordinary environments in which to live, work, study, shop, dine, and play. Their work has been published in Canada, the US, England, and Japan, and has been featured in several television productions.

Index by architect